786

'Aqaaid of the Muslim

Shaikh 'Abdul Mustafa

"'Aqaaid of the Muslim"

© 2013 Shaikh 'Abdul Mustafa'. All rights reserved.

ISBN 978-0-9575442-2-2

Published by Shaikh 'Abdul Mustafa
051113

www.MuslimAqeeda.com

(Printed in India)

Bismillaah...

This Book is dedicated to all those who
sincerely seek the truth

Contents

عقائد المسلم

شيخ عبد المصطفى

Introduction

By the majesty of the Almighty and the love of His beloved worshippers, we are honoured to be able to present this book on the *Aqaaid* (fundamental beliefs) of the Muslim. We have cited references to prove that each point made is from Qur'an and *sunnah* and thus has validity, purpose and necessity in belief.

It is easy to object or criticise because one doesn't wish to understand something. Arrogance and ignorance can lead quickly to disbelief so we should be sincere in accepting the truth when it challenges our misconceptions. The Holy Qur'an must be our first guide in this. Allah^{swt} states that His revelation is a clear book which contains all knowledge:

> "And we revealed to you the Qur'an that is an account of everything"
> *(Holy Qur'an 16:89)*

> "...and it is a clear book..." *(Holy Qur'an 15:5 & 27:1)*

Thus we first turn to the Glorious Qur'an to guide us – as we have done in this book for every question & answer. We must also accept the teachings of our beloved Prophet Muhammad^S, who has stated that the true knowledge and practice will always be with the majority (*jamaa'ah*):

> "Allah will never allow my *Ummah* to unite upon misguidance and incorrect beliefs..." (*Tirmithi 2,173*)

Thus, let's agree to be guided by the Qur'an, *ahadith* and the majority, or should we remain ignorant of the truth?

We have intentionally limited each answer to a double page for ease of reference and tried to keep each section independent, even though numerous additional references and arguments exist. These are available on our website 'www.MuslimAqeeda.com'. Unfortunately in this book we have had to leave out the Arabic for briefness. A glossary of terms is included as is a brief synopsis on each of the references quoted.

We make *du'a* that Almighty Allah accepts this effort and our beloved Prophet Muhammad^S is pleased with this and approves with his blessings and continuous guidance, *ameen*.

1

1   Qs: Is Allah^{swt} everywhere?

Answer: Yes, Allah^{swt} is everywhere in His attributes and essence without being any part of His Creation. To say He is not everywhere limits His Majesty.

Evidence from Holy Qur'an

"And He is Allah in the heavens and in the earth..." *Holy Qur'an (6:3)*

Clearly, Allah is <u>everywhere</u> in the heavens and in the earth. This should be evidence enough. But to continue further:

"To Allah belongs the East and the West, and wherever you turn, behold the face of Allah" *Holy Qur'an (2:115)*

In this verse above, Allah^{swt} tells the reader that He is in every direction, left, right, up, down, forwards and backwards. So whichever way you turn (to pray *salah* or make *du'a*), you are definitely facing your Lord. Thus, Allah^{swt} is everywhere in His creation. He perceives everything that is taking place anywhere in the Universe and actually encompasses and surrounds the entirety of the Creation. The Almighty says:

"Allah encompasses everything" *Holy Qur'an (4:126)*

How does Allah^{swt} encompass everything and is everywhere? We don't know because our limited intellect cannot comprehend Him:

"There is nothing like Him" *Holy Qur'an (42:11)*

He is nothing like the Creation and the understanding of His existence is beyond our comprehension as we can only think within the laws He has created – but He is above those laws. Thus He is everywhere in His creation without being a part of it or dependent upon it.

Evidence from *Ahadith*

"Allah the Almighty said: ...I am with my worshipper when he remembers me..." *(Bukhari 93:502)*

In this *hadith*, if a person mentions his Lord, or performs his *thikr* (remembrance) then wherever he may be, Allah^{swt} is with him.

Without elaborating on the mechanics of this divine presence it means Allah[swt] is everywhere as if a Muslim is performing *thikr* in Alaska, Japan or even on the moon, Allah[swt] is with all of them – wherever they may be in the Creation. In another hadith (known as *hadithe-Jaariyah*), a servant girl was asked by Prophet Muhammad[S]:

'Where is Allah?' (*ayn Allah*) and she said, 'In Heaven.' *(Muslim 7:33)*

Clearly, Allah[swt] is not only in His creation, but he is also in Heaven. In fact, *Muhaditheen*, explain this as referring to the direction of our *du'a* (i.e. her *du'a* is not to idols). This *hadith* does not say Allah is not everywhere or only limited to heaven. So, Allah[swt] is everywhere, and there is no limit whatsoever to Him being in one place or another for if there were then he would be an attribute of creation which is not the case.

Discussion

People often accuse that to believe Allah[swt] is everywhere, is to believe He is a part of the Creation. They are further confused by thinking that if Allah[swt] is everywhere then Allah[swt] is everything. This is totally wrong and has no basis in Islam.

By understanding the proofs provided, the Muslim is elevated to a higher understanding of the reality of Allah[swt]. That, first and foremost as the Creator He is like nothing in the Creation. Furthermore, Allah[swt] exists in a way that the physical brain can never fully comprehend. He is everywhere in His attributes and His essence but we don't know how.

Once a Muslim realises that Allah[swt] is everywhere, in every direction without actually being a part of Creation then they have truly understood *tawheed* (oneness) of Allah[swt]. After all, due to our limited intellect there is no logical way to understand Allah[swt] – who is unlimited. We can only go by Allah's verses to understand His Majesty. There is not a single piece of evidence that says Allah is not everywhere, only conjecture based upon ignorance. Allah Almighty is definitely everywhere as He states and as His beloved Messenger[S] states.

3

2

Qs: Those people who do *sajdah* to graves, aren't they grave worshippers and Mushriks?

Answer: To do *sajdah* to anyone or anything other than Allah[swt] is *haram*. It can only be classified as *shirk* if the person doing *sajdah* does so with the intention of 'worship'.

Evidence from Holy Qur'an

"And we said to the Angels, do *sajdah* to Adam. They bowed down except Iblees who refused out of pride and he was amongst the disbelievers." *(Holy Qur'an 2:34)*

Sajdah is prostration of a person's head on the ground. In this case, those who did not do *sajdah* were classified by Allah[swt] as *kaafireen* (unbelievers).

From this verse it is clear that *sajdah* was allowed in times gone past, but this was *sajdah* out of respect and not worship. Allah[swt] would not allow *shirk* under any circumstances. This then proves that *sajdah* of worship is different to *sajdah* of respect. *Sajdah* out of false worship takes a person out of Islam as it is *haram* and *shirk*. *Sajdah* out of respect used to be allowed as clearly demonstrated by the above verse. Doing *sajdah* out of respect is *haram* for us and causes someone to be sinful although still be a Muslim.

Evidence from *Ahadith*

"Actions are judged according to intentions." *(Bukhari 1)*

Our beloved Prophet Muhammad[S] has indicated that a person's intentions are essential in determining the actions and consequences of such actions. This then reinforces that if someone does *sajdah* to anything other than Allah, to call that person a *mushrik* could be wrong. That person should be stopped and told that it is a sin and that it should not be done again. If someone automatically shouts *kaafir!* or *mushrik!*, then we need to be aware of the following *hadith*:

"If one Muslim calls another Muslim a *kaafir*, then one of them is definitely a *kaafir*." *(Bukhari 5,752)*

4

So it is extremely dangerous to use the words '*kaafir*' and '*mushrik*' to other Muslims as a person's own *iman* (belief) could be affected:

Ibn Majah narrated that 'Abd-Allaah Ibn Abi Awfa[R] said: "When Mu'adh came from Syria, he prostrated to the Prophet[S] who said, 'What is this, O Mu'adh?' He said, 'I went to Syria and saw them prostrating to their archbishops and patriarchs, and I wanted to do that for you.' The Messenger[S] of Allah said, 'Do not do that. If I were to command anyone to prostrate to anyone other than Allah, I would have commanded women to prostrate to their husbands.' *(Ibn Majah 1,853)*

Clearly Hazrat Mu'adh[R] was not asked to repeat his *shahaadah*, nor was he told he was committing shirk but rather was corrected by Prophet Muhammad[S] very calmly and very beautifully.

Discussion

"Grave worship" is a common accusation against people visiting graves. The Prophet Muhammad[S] said:

"I forbade you from visiting graves, but now visit them." *(Abu Daood 3,689, Muslim 2,131)*

People have intentionally confused *visiting* graves with *worshipping* graves. Worshipping graves (or worshipping anything other than Allah[swt]) is *shirk* but visiting them is the instruction of our beloved Prophet Muhammad[S]. It is noteworthy that Prophet Muhammad[S] also indicated that he did not fear *shirk* for his people:

"...By Allah I do not fear that you associate others with Allah after me, but I fear you will fight for worldly things" *(Bukhari 1,344, Muslim 2,296)*

So if Prophet Muhammad[S] did not fear *shirk*, why are certain Muslims so concerned - or do they know better than our beloved Prophet[S]? Once a person accepts Islam they recognise and worship the one, true *ilah* or 'god' who is Allah[swt]. They know the meaning of *kalimah tayyibah* (the first *kalimah*) and know the meaning and definition of *shirk*. One should not belittle the meaning, understanding and authority of *kalimah tayyibah*:

"There is no god except Allah,
Muhammad[S] is the Messenger of Allah."

5

3

Qs: Asking help from anyone other than Allah^{swt} is shirk (*Surah Fatiha* verse 4) isn't it?

Answer: No - you can ask help from anyone pious - living or dead - as long as you believe that the help ultimately is from Allah^{swt} and that the individual helping you is Allah's creation.

Evidence from Holy Qur'an

"Ask from the people of *thikr* (those who remember Allah) if you don't know." *(Holy Qur'an 16:43)*

In this verse Allah^{swt} instructs us to ask from those who remember him i.e. those have religious knowledge and practice that knowledge. These are scholars have been gifted by the Almighty to impart guidance to the general public – and this verse is not limited to those who are alive. *Hazrat* Sulaiman^A said:

"O court members which one of you can bring me her throne before they come humbled in my presence...The one with knowledge of the book said, 'I will bring it to you within the twinkling of an eye' " *(HQ 27:38-40)*

From this it shows that *Hazrat* Sulaiman <u>asked help</u> from his assembly, and in the end a man with knowledge of the book brought it within the blinking of an eye. Additionally, a Jinn also offered to bring the throne. Why didn't hazrat Suleiman ask directly from Allah^{swt} and why does Allah^{swt} quote this story? Thus, *Hazrat* Sulaiman^A asked for help, a Jinn offered help and a man gave help. Thus a prophet, a Jinn, a man and Allah^{swt} himself all declare and demonstrate that asking Allah's creation for help is permissible and recommended.

Now if we are to look at verse 4 in surah *Fatiha*:

"Thee alone we worship and thee alone we ask for help." *(HQ 1:4)*

This means that we worship Allah^{swt} as the only true god that we can ask for help. In the past people asked idols for help – believing they were gods - and it is this aspect of *shirk* (asking false gods for help) that the verse is referring to. Thus, asking any other than

6

Allah^swt for help – knowing that they are Allah's creation - is totally permissible.

Evidence from *Ahadith*

> The Blessed Prophet^S said to *Sayyidina* Ka'ab^R, "ask for something?" Ka'ab^R said, "I ask for your companionship in *Jannah*." The Holy Prophet^S replied, "Do you want something else?" and Ka'ab^R replied, "Just this" so the Prophet^S said, "co-operate with me by doing more prostrations". *(Muslim 990)*

In this *hadith*, the companion asked the holy Prophet^S for *jannah* and the holy Prophet^S did not say, 'you can't ask anyone for help except Allah - you are a *mushrik* and cannot ask me for jannah' rather, the prophet^S asked if the companion wanted anything else. In another *hadith Sayyidina* Anas bin Malik^R narrated:

> Certainly, Umar^R bin Al-Khattab^R whenever drought threatened them used to ask Abbas bin Abdul Muttalib^R to invoke Allah for rain. He used to say, 'O Allah! We have been (continuously) invoking you for rain through the Prophet^S and you would bless us with rain, and now we ask you through the uncle of your prophet. 'O Allah! Bless us with rain', he said, and so it would rain.' *(Bukhari 1,010)*

Hazrat 'Umar^R did not ask directly from Allah^swt, but he went through the Prophet Muhammad^S and through *Hazrat* Abbas^R. He could have easily performed *salatul Istisqaa* (prayer for rain) himself but instead, chose to ask others for help proving that this method is totally permissible and is the *sunnah* of the companions^R.

Discussion

In the concept of 'thee alone we worship and thee alone, we ask for help', 'asking' is not restricted to Allah^swt only, but the acceptance that Allah^swt is the ultimate provider – the *ilaah* (true God). Others can also be asked. The verse (16:43) mentioned before instructs us to ask for help from those humans who have knowledge and practice and shows it is an important and essential part of Islam.

Thus we can go directly to Allah^swt and we can go to other people to ask help. Did not Allah^swt send humanity 124,000 prophets to guide us and for us to ask their help? In this alone there are 124,000 evidences for all time.

4

Qs: What is the evidence of sending *salah* (blessings) and *salam* (peace, i.e. *salat-us-salam*) to Prophet Muhammad^S?

Answer: Allah^{swt} himself orders Muslims to send *salah* and *salam* (blessings and peace) and so did Prophet Muhammad^S so instruct.

Evidence from Holy Qur'an

"Indeed, Allah and His angels shower blessings on the Prophet. O you who believe send blessing on him and send peace on him submissively."
Holy Qur'an (33:56)

This verse informs us the act of sending *salah* (*drood*) and *salaam* upon the Prophet^S is such a special act that it is one which Allah^{swt} Himself and His noble angels perform to honour the Holy Prophet^S. It is thus one of the most highest and praiseworthy acts in Islam. Allah^{swt} does not have to do this but wants to and wants his Angels to. He also orders those who believe to send peace and blessings as well and to send them respectfully and humbly.

When Allah^{swt} sends peace upon the Holy Prophet^S, He is blessing him. When Muslims and Angels send peace (salutations), they are actually showing Almighty Allah their respect for the Holy Prophet^S. For believers it is also a supplication through which our sins are forgiven and our status is increased in this world and in the hereafter. As this is a direct commandment from Allah^{swt}, then not performing this action is disobeying one's Lord and Creator and is sinful. To argue against it is also sinful.

Evidence from *Hadith*:

The Messenger of Allah said: 'Whoever sends one *salah* (*drood*) upon me, Allah will send ten upon him.' *(Muslim 4:747)*

In this *hadith*, the Prophet^S is legitimising the act of the believers sending *salah* and *salaam* to himself and informing us of the virtues of doing so. There are numerous *ahadith* that advise us of the merits of sending *salah* and *salaam* in different ways, expressions and numbers and all of them extolling the merits of doing so for a believer's *imaan*. In a further *hadith*, the actual need to perform this act is highlighted quite clearly in terms of not only how virtuous it is but also its benefits to the believer as narrated by *Sayyidina* 'Umar bin al Khattab[R].

"Indeed the supplication (*du'a*), hangs between the heavens and the earth until you send *Salah* on your Prophet[S]." (*Tirmithi 21:486*)

"A supplication remains suspended between heaven and earth and does not ascend any further until a person sends *salah* on me....send *salah* upon me at the beginning of your supplication, at the end, and in the middle." (*Jami al-Usool by Razin ibn Mu'awiyah*)

Clearly Allah[swt] wants us to honour our Prophet Muhammad[S] even when making *du'a* to Him. He causes the *du'a* to hang until we honour the name of his beloved, Prophet Muhammad[S].

"The one who sends *salah* on me, Allah will write for him 10 rewards, forgive 10 of his sins, and elevate him by 10 levels." (*Nisaai 3:50, Ahmad 102 & 261, Mustadrak 1:550*)

Incredible! Sending just one blessing on our beloved Prophet Muhammad[S], gives us such amazing gifts from Allah[swt], which shows how much importance our Creator gives this blessed act.

"The closest of mankind to me on the day of judgement is he who sends me most *salah* (blessings)." (*Tirmithi 482:21*)

It is now clear how much blessing is there in sending *salah* and *salam* on Prophet Muhammad[S]. It is one of the easiest ways of earning reward if we wish but more importantly, it allows us to become close to our Prophet Muhammad[S]. Only an absolute fool would have problem with this.

Discussion

The evidence for sending *salah* and *salam* to the Prophet[S] is clear, and unambiguous. In fact it is an order, but one which is full of blessings for us, both now and on the day of judgement. Only someone who dislikes the prophet Muhammad[S] would dislike sending blessing on him or object to the same. It is not the blessed Prophet Muhammad[S] who needs us to send him *salah* and *salam*, but we need the blessings associated with such an action.

9

5 Qs: Why should you stand up for the Holy Prophet[S] in reading *salaat-us-salaam (blessings & peace).*

Answer: Standing up while offering *salaat-us-salaam* is totally permissible, desirable and highly recommended (*mustahab*) as it is a sign of respect, honour and love for our beloved Prophet[S].

Evidence from Holy Qur'an

"And whoso respects the signs of Allah, then it is from piety of the heart."
(Holy Qur'an 22:32)

The greatest sign of Allah[swt] is the Holy Prophet[S]. Allah[swt] has made the sending of blessings and salutations upon his messenger compulsory upon believers (see Chapter 4) just as He has made the love, honour and respect for the Holy prophet compulsory upon believers. He clearly states:

"That you (people) believe in Allah and his messenger and honour and respect the messenger and exalt Allah morning and afternoon". *(Holy Qur'an 48:9)*

We stand up for the Holy Prophet[S] as a sign of respect love and honour. Sending salutations and blessings upon him is one of the most virtuous acts a believer can do.

Evidence from *Ahadith*

Hazrat Abu Huraira[R] narrates: 'The Holy Prophet[S] was seated with us in the mosque and speaking to us. When he rose to depart we all rose up with him and remained standing until he entered one of the houses of his wives.' *(Sunan Abu Daood, Mishkaat 47:57)*

This *hadith* shows how much the companions would show utmost respect for the Holy Prophet[S]. Standing up was a sign of love respect and honour and they stood up for him and he never stopped them.

Abu Saidi al Kudri[R] narrates "The people of Banu Quraiza agreed to accept the verdict of Sa'ad bin Muadhr, so the Prophet[S] send for Sa'ad[R], and the latter came riding on a donkey, as he approached, the Holy

10

Prophet^S said, 'Stand up for your leader or for the best amongst you.'
(Bukhari 477)

If *Hazrat Sa'ad*^R is worthy of such honour and the command is coming from the holy Prophet^S, then consider the position of the holy Prophet^S himself. Clearly, we should get up and honour him while sending blessings and salutations upon Him. *Hazrat Sa'ad*^R was the chief of *Banu Quraiza* and the Holy Prophet^S is his chief, our chief, our leader and our master. As he has instructed us to stand up for our betters and leaders, then we are duty-bound to stand up for our beloved Prophet Muhammad^S. Or do we ignore this instruction and make feeble excuses?

Out of extreme love for *hazrat* Fatima^R the holy Prophet^S would stand up for her kiss her and make her sit where he was sitting when she would visit him, and *hazrat* Fatima^R would do the same when holy Prophet^S would visit her. *(Abu Daood 5,175)*

Discussion

Standing up for someone is both civilised and respectful. Thus it is the most appropriate way to show honour and respect when sending *salatus-salam* (blessings and peace) upon the Holy Prophet^S. The Prophet^S himself instructed us in *Bukhari* to stand up for our leaders and for those better than us. He is our leader and who else is better than Prophet Muhammad^S?

Standing out of respect and honour is not something new or disapproved of in Islam. The companions would stand for holy Prophet^S as he would depart from the gathering and when he would approach as a sign of respect, love and honour.

When Muslims read *salatul-janaza* we have to recite *durood* upon the holy Prophet^S in a standing position. If standing up (*qiyam*) and reciting *drood* was not allowed surely we wouldn't have been allowed to recite *janaza* in this way? We are still required to follow this. If people do not wish to stand up whilst reciting *drood*, then they need to advise as to which other way is better. Also, they should not stop others from respecting the greatest of Allah's signs and the greatest of Allah's creation.

6 Qs: Prove that you can say *"yaa Rasoolallah"* (O Messenger of Allah) as *"yaa"* should only be for those alive and close by.

Answer: To proclaim *yaa Rasoolullah* is permissible whether near or far, during his lifetime and after his demise.

Evidence from Holy Qur'an

"O Prophet, (*yaa ayu han nabiyy*) verily we have sent you as a witness, giver of glad tidings and a Warner" *(Holy Qur'an 33:45)*

Verily to call the Holy Prophet[S] by way of *"yaa"* (*nidaa* in grammar) is proven from the verses of the Holy Qur'an. Allah[swt] addresses His Messenger[S] in such a fashion:

"O thou wrapped up..." (*yaa ayuhal muzzamil, Holy Qur'an 73:1*).

"O thou wrapped up..." (*yaa, ayuhal muddathir, Holy Qur'an 74:1*)

All these verses show how lovingly Allah[swt] calls Prophet Muhammad[S], not by his blessed name, but by his blessed titles, using the word '*yaa*'. Whenever we read the Holy Qur'an we repeat these words and thus call respectfully upon the Prophet Muhammad[S].

Evidence from *Ahadith*

Sayyidinaa Abdullahi ibn Umar[R] once suffered from a cramp, someone advised him to remember the person whom he loved the most, he proclaimed loudly '*Yaa* Muhammad[S], and he was immediately relieved. *(al adab muf'rad hadith 964)*

This was the practice of the pious predecessors, not only did they proclaim the name of the holy Prophet[S] by addressing him with *"yaa"*, but they would make intercession with his name to be cured. And they were cured.

Sayyidina 'Uthman bin Hunaif[R] related: "A blind man came to the holy Prophet[S] and said pray to me so that I recover my eyesight, our beloved Prophet[S] said "perform good *wudu*, offer two *rak'ah* of prayer then say, 'O Allah, I ask you through my Prophet Muhammad[S], the Prophet of mercy, O Muhammad[S] (*yaa Muhammad*), I seek your intercession with my Lord for my eyesight." *(Tirmithi –127:589, nr 3,589 [1])* Imam Baihaqqi added, *Sayyidina* 'Uthman[R] said, 'we were not separated yet and it was not long, the blind man returned to us as if he was never blind. *(Shifaa siqaam).*

The blessed companions[R] used to use this phrase '*yaa Muhammad*[S]' in the prophets presence, in his absence and after his passing away. This was instructed by the blessed Prophet[S] himself!

Sayyidina Zainab the sister of Imam Hussein proclaimed "yaa Muhammad" at Karbala *(al badaya wanahaya vol 8 page 193).* After the demise of Umar al Farooq[R] in 18AH, there was a severe drought due to which *hazrat* Bilaal bin al Harith said "*yaa Muhammad*" *(al-badaya wa nahaya vol 7 p.91)*

Sayyidina Ali bin Abu Talib[R], narrated: I was with the Prophet[S] in Makkah. We came out to its outskirts. We did not pass any mountain or tree except that it said, "peace be on you O Messenger of Allah." *(As-salaamu 'alaika yaa Rasoolallah) (Tirmithi 50:8, nr 3,646).*

Subhanallah! The mountains and trees are better than us at respecting the beloved Prophet[S].

In another narration of *Othman bin Hanif*[R] a man came to the *khalifa* way after the demise of the holy Prophet[S] and was told to supplicate with the above *du'a* of the blind companion and his needs were fulfilled. *(Mujmal kabeer lil tibraani 8,232).*

Discussion

Allah[swt] declares the word *yaa* frequently when calling our beloved Prophet Muhammad[S]. It was also the practice of the companions and those who followed after them to proclaim the words," *Yaa Muhammad*[S] *and Yaa Rasoolullah*[S] whilst he was alive and after his demise. This was based upon the Prophet's[S] own instructions.

Daily, all Muslims recite *attahiyaat* in their daily prayers which contains the ever blissful phrase '*assalaamu alaika ayuha nabiy'* and *ayuha* and *yaa* are the same, meaning 'O Messenger[S]. So even those who object – they recite it! So, proclaiming *"Yaa"* for *Rasoolullah*[S] is practiced by Allah[swt], instructed by Prophet Muhammad[S] himself, practiced by the noble companions[R] and thus is totally permissible and not an innovation in Islam.

13

7   Qs: Is the holy Prophet^S *haadir* (present) and *naazir* (seeing)?

Answer   It is fact that the holy Prophet^S is *Haadir* and *Naathir* (through Allah's power) and he can see, hear whatever he wishes and be present anywhere and at any time he wishes.

Evidence from Holy Qur'an

> "O my Prophet, verily we have sent you as a Witness, giver of glad tidings and a Warner..." (*Holy Qur'an 33:45*)

The meaning of witness (*shaahid*) is one who sees, hears and knows. Allah^{swt} has repeated this title in many verses in the holy Qur'an. The attributes of the holy Prophet^S are active attributes. A witness clearly requires one to be present, seeing and hearing to testify in any court of law. Surely if this title of 'witness' is given by the Almighty Himself, then it must mean a comprehensive and perfect witness. To suggest anything else implies a person doesn't believe in this clear verse with a clear meaning or are they trying to accuse Allah^{swt} of choosing the wrong wording? Not only is the holy Prophet^S a witness for his *ummah* but for other previous nations and <u>all mankind</u> as well:

> "We have made you a justly balanced ummah, so that you may be a witness over mankind and the messenger is a witness over all of you..."
> *(Holy Qur'an 2:143)*

His position as a 'witness' is totally clear - he sees, hears and knows. Additionally:

> "The Prophet is closer to the believers than their own souls." *(HQ 33:6)*

Clearly, he is closer to us than even our own souls. Let's be honest, our souls are pretty close, physically and spiritually and they are an integral part of us - and he is closer than that! Thus, he is close to every believer in this world and in *barzakh* (afterlife).

For someone to be so close means he is witnessing everything and already knows an amount that is unimaginable.

Evidence from ahadith

Hazrat Abdullah bin Umar[R] narrates that the holy Prophet[S] said, "Allah has raised the entire world in front of me so that I can observe anything in it, and everything that will take place from now until the day of judgement, just as I see the palm of my hand..." (*Kanzul 'Ummaal 31,810 & similar in Baihaqqi 18,617*)

Clearly, he has the power to see or hear anything he wishes in any place and in any time.

The beloved Prophet[S] said, 'My life is beneficial for you as you talk to me and I talk to you. When I pass away, my demise is also beneficial for you, your deeds will be presented to me and if see goodness I will praise Allah and if I see badness I will ask forgiveness for you.' (*Tabaqaatul Kubraa 2:194*)

In this *hadith* it is clear that the holy Prophet[S] watches our deeds, seeks forgiveness for us and sees our spiritual progress. Thus he sees any person he wishes and their deeds as well. With 1.5 billion Muslims present on this earth, if we assume he is seeing their deeds once per week (*Abu Daood 1,531*) then he would be seeing the deeds of 2,500 people per second! Amazing *mashaAllah*.

Discussion

It is easy for people to believe that the devil is with everyone but those with weak faith have difficulty believing that the Prophet[S] is more powerful than that. Allah[swt] gave his Prophet[S] the quality of being *shaahid* (witness) and gave him power to be in different places at different times. This is clearly evident from Qur'an and *hadith*.

Also every person when being questioned in the grave is blessed with the vision of seeing the Prophet[S] whether a believer or not. The question is how many people die every second? At least 4 people per second all over the world. Plus many are blessed with his presence in their dreams. About this the Prophet[S] states that: 'whoever sees me in a dream has indeed seen me in reality.' (*Muslim 5,635, Bukhari 6,594*). Plus he is receiving our deeds. Thus he is in so many places - *Haadir* (present) and *Naathir* (seeing) - and there is no doubt.

15

8

Qs: How can you say the holy Prophet[S] was light when he was clearly a human being?

Answer: The reality of the holy Prophet[S] is certainly light (*noor*) and he is also the greatest of human beings.

Evidence from Holy Qur'an

"There has come to you from Allah a light and a clear book." *(Holy Qur'an 5:15)*

All commentators of the holy Qur'an have referred the 'light' in this verse to be the holy Prophet[S]. Allah[swt] says:

"Allah is the light of the heavens and the earth. The example of His light *(noor)* is as a niche in which is a lamp…" *(Holy Qur'an 24:35)*

Regarding this verse the greatest commentator of Qur'an *Abdullah ibn Abbas*[R] says the second light refers to the holy Prophet[S]. *(As-Shifa p.6)*. The lamp in the niche is narrated to be the blessed heart of Prophet Muhammad[S] in his blessed chest - further demonstrating the intensity and comprehensiveness of his blessed light. Later in the verse, he is further described as:

"…light upon light…" *(Holy Qur'an 24:35)*

Not just light – but light upon light. How much more clearer does the Holy Qur'an have to be? We need to accept the description and statement of Allah[swt] and as confirmed by all the great *Mufassiroon*.

"We sent you as a witness, giver of glad tidings and a Warner, one who calls to Allah with his permission and a lamp radiating with light." *(Holy Qur'an 33: 46)*

In this verse Allah[swt] addresses his Messenger[S] as a light that's shining so brightly, it is giving out tremendous amount of light.

Evidence from *Ahadith*

Sayyidina Jabir bin Abdullah[R] asked: 'O messenger of Allah, may my father and mother be sacrificed for you. Please inform me about the first thing Almighty Allah created. He said: 'O Jaabir, certainly, Almighty Allah, before anything else, created the light of your Prophet from His light. Then that light began to go around wherever almighty Allah willed.' ...*(Sharh Az-Zurqaani volume1 pages 89-91).*

This *hadith* is clear in that beloved Prophet Muhammad[S] is light and he is created from the light of Allah[swt]. As a first step, this reality should be accepted. How this occurred is beyond our comprehension and beyond our understanding of physical laws. There are further *ahadith* proving the physicality of his blessed light:

Sayyidina Anas bin Malik[R] narrates, 'The day when the holy prophet entered Madina, everything in it was illuminated through his *noor*, and when he passed away everything in it became dark'. *(Tirmithi 3,638)*

The companions asked the holy prophet, 'O Messenger of Allah inform us about yourself. The holy Prophet[S] said 'I am the prayer of my father *Ibrahim*[A], I am the tiding of *Isa*[A], when my mother was pregnant with me, she saw that a *noor* emerged from her which made her see Syria. *(al-Mustadrak 4,174)*

Sayyidina *'Ali*[R] said, 'When the holy Prophet[S] would speak, light (noor) used to be seen emerging from his blessed teeth.' (*Mawahib lidunya [2]*)

Discussion

The above evidences give crystal clear proof of the light (*noor*) of the holy Prophet[S]. The companions[R] lived with him, observed him, saw him eating and drinking etc but they still accepted him to be *noor*. None of the companions would address the holy Prophet[S] in the same way they addressed other human beings as they realized and appreciated his special nature and incredible position. Even modern science believes that all particles have a wavelength and light can behave as particles (wave-particle duality theory).

Every Muslim knows that *hazrat* Jibraeel[A] is made out of light *(Muslim 7,134)* but can also come in the form of a human being *(Bukhari 47, Muslim 4)*. Therefore, it is not beyond even a simple person's comprehension that light and humanity can co-exist. The greatest companions and Qur'anic commentators ascribed *noor* to the holy Prophet[S]. His essence is *noor* (light) and his reality is a combination of matter and light. Clarity upon clarity, proof upon proof – light upon light!

17

9

Qs: **Prophet Muhammad^S was a normal, mortal man who came to deliver a message and nothing more. We should respect him as an elder brother or fatherly figure only.**

Answer: No. The holy Prophet^S is the greatest of creation. It is prohibited to portray him as just an 'ordinary human being', reducing his status and authority.

Evidence from Holy Qur'an

"Say (O Muhammad), I am a man for your example, it is revealed to me that your Lord is one" *(Holy Qur'an 18:110)*.

In this verse there is no denial of the concept of the Prophet^S as a human being but not an ordinary human being, certainly not 'like us'. Some translate this verse wrongly as 'I am a man like you' which is incorrect as the word *'mithlukum'* means for 'your example' and not 'like you'. The verse further explains that he receives revelation, so we cannot be 'like him' or do we receive revelation as well? In fact, we shouldn't refer to the Prophet's as 'men like us' at all as the disbelievers would use such language, just as the people of Nuh^A for example:

"The chiefs who disbelieved among his people said, we do not see you except a man like ourselves" *(Holy Qur'an 11:27)*

Such degrading comments of the Prophets^A caused destruction to many nations before us. There are huge differences between ordinary humans and special humans like Prophets^A and Messengers^A. In regards to the holy Prophet^S, he is the most perfect and most unique of all human beings. Besides being an amazing light (*noor*) he is sent as mercy to the entire universe *(HQ 21:107)* and as a witness over all other nations *(HQ 2:143)*.

"Whoever obeys the messenger indeed obeys Allah" *(HQ 4:79)*

The obedience of the Messenger^S is the obedience of Allah^{swt}. Which other human is like this? This makes him the most perfect example whom we can't compare to ourselves or to anyone else. To try and find faults or weaknesses goes totally against Qur'an and reality– as he has not got any faults or weaknesses.

Evidence from *Ahadith*

Said the Prophet[S]: "By the one whose hand contains my soul - None of you believes until I become dearer to them than their parents, children, and everyone else." *(Bukhari 14 & 15)*

Clearly, the Prophet Muhammad[S] was and is NOT 'a man like anyone' as we have to love him more than anyone else. Additionally:

The Prophet[S] said, "Do not practice *Al-Wisaal* (fasting continuously without break)." The people said to the Prophet[S], "But you practice *Al-Wisaal*?" The Prophet[S] replied, "<u>Are you like me?</u> I am given food and drink (by Allah) during the night." *(Bukhari 31:182)*.

The beloved Companions[R] were not able to copy the holy Prophet[S] in his continuous fasting and he forbade them from doing so. It is evident from this authentic *ahadith* that the holy Prophet[S] is not like anyone as he said so himself.

Hazrat Abbas[R] narrates that the holy Prophet[S] said 'Allah created creation, and <u>made me the best of it</u>...Then He chose tribes and made me from the best tribe. Then He chose families and made me from the best family. So <u>I am the best of them</u> from the best family.' *(Tirmithi 3,627 [3])*

Sayyidina Ali[R] said. "I have not seen anybody similar to the holy Prophet[S] either before or after." *(Tarikh kabeer, Tirmithi 3,570)*.

Discussion

In the light of Qur'an and *Sunnah* Allah[swt] clearly prohibits us from addressing the holy Prophet[S] as a 'man like us'. This was a practise of those who belied messengers of Allah[swt]. The companions[R] honoured him in such a way that his beloved saliva was a cure for their sicknesses, his perspiration was the best of all perfumes, even his blood was pure for them *(Bukhari 52:192)* and they would compete for his used water after ablution. Not an ordinary human.

He is a Prophet[S] and Messenger of Allah and receives revelation. So, he is definitely not 'like us' (as we are weak, pathetic and sinful), but he is the best of humans, the best of creation and the closest to Allah[swt], peace and blessing be upon him, always.

19

10   Qs: How can you say that the holy Prophet^S can benefit us now he has passed away and is buried in Madina?

Answer: The help of the Prophet^S upon his *ummah* is not restricted to life and death. He is alive and continues to be our Prophet^S.

Evidence from Holy Qur'an

"We sent not the messenger, but to be obeyed in accordance with the will of Allah. If they were unjust to themselves (sinned) <u>they should go to you</u> (messenger) and ask Allah's forgiveness and the messenger also asks forgiveness for them, they would find Allah most forgiving most merciful. *(Holy Qur'an 4:64)*

This is a divine order to seek help and intercession of the holy Prophet^S. The verse is not restricted to time (*mutlaq*) as then the Holy Qur'an becomes a limited book. If it is restricted to place then the path of forgiveness for sinners will be for only those present in Madina. This is unjust and the Prophet^S is the most just and close to all of us who believe:

"The messenger is closer to the believers than even their own selves (or souls)". *(Holy* Qur'an *33:4)*

Thus, the order to go to Prophet Muhammad^S, becomes clearer as he is extremely close to those who believe. Thus calling him and asking him for help and *du'a* becomes comprehensible.

"Verily your helper is Allah, his messenger and the believers..."
(Holy Qur'an 5:55)

The above verse establishes that after Allah^{swt}, the holy Prophet^S is our helper even now. Similarly all the pious have the ability to help us even from their graves as Allah^{swt} does not place a restriction. (Please also see chapter 21).

Evidence from *Ahadith*

Hazrat Abdullah Ibn Mas'ood narrated that the Messenger of Allah said, 'My life is good for you, you talk to me and I talk to you, and my demise is good for you. Your actions will be presented to me (in my grave) and if I see goodness I will praise Allah, and if I see other than that I will ask forgiveness of him (for you). *(at tabqatul kubra 2:194)*

Even now the holy Prophet[S] is watching us and making du'a for us – *Subhanallah!* This further proves his closeness and the fact that the office of prophet-hood continues.

Abu al-Jawza' Aws bin 'Abdullah narrates: The people of Medina were in the grip of a severe famine. They complained to 'Aisha (about their terrible condition). She told them to go towards the grave of the Prophet[S] and open a window in the direction of the sky so that there is no curtain between the sky and the grave. They did so. Then it started raining heavily - even the lush green grass sprang up (everywhere) and the camels had grown so fat (it seemed) they would burst. So the year was named as the year of greenery and plenty. *(Daarimi 93)*

It was clearly the practice of the noble companions[R] to seek help from the grave of the prophet Muhammad[S]. So why the objection today?

Sayyidina Abdullahi ibn Umar once suffered from a cramp, someone advised him to remember the person whom he loved the most, he proclaimed loudly *"Yaa Muhammad!"*, and he was immediately relieved. *(al adab muf'rad hadith 964)*. This was after the demise of the holy Prophet[S] and shows how the companions used to call for his blessed help despite the fact he is in *barzakh*.

Discussion

It is easy for people to believe that *Iblees* (Satan) can affect all of us by whispering to misguide us. But when it comes to the power of the greatest of creation, why do some struggle in appreciating the powers and the abilities of Prophet Muhammad[S]?

Kalimah tayyiba states that Muhammad[S] is the Messenger of Allah, not 'was'. The office prophet-hood is continuing. As our prophet he is watching us and praying for us. He can still and is still benefitting us. Whenever the noble companions would go through extreme difficulties they would turn to the holy Prophet[S] wherever they were and their needs were fulfilled. Thus calling upon him for help is totally permissible and indeed desirable and he continues to be our Prophet[S].

11 Qs: Prophet Muhammad^S has passed away, why do you say he is alive?

Answer: The prophet Muhammad^S is definitely alive although we cannot fully understand how.

Evidence from Holy Qur'an

"And say not of those who are killed in the way of Allah they are dead, indeed they are alive but you do not understand". *(Holy Qur'an 2:154)*

Clearly, all who have been killed in Allah's way are not dead. Allah^{swt} is the one who defines life and death – not us. So, we are not allowed to say that these people are 'dead'. The Prophet Muhammad^S, is the greatest of creation and hence the greatest of the martyrs and hence we are not allowed to say he is dead, but he is alive.

"Think not of those who are killed in Allah's way as dead. No, they are alive, receiving sustenance from the presence of their Lord.
(Holy Qur'an 3:169)

We can't even think of martyrs as dead. Hence, we are not even allowed to think that the Prophet Muhammad^S is dead. Anyone who does is disobeying Allah's commandment.

The above two *Ayahs* were revealed after the Battle of *Badr*. The noble companions^R used to feel sorry for those who lost their lives in the battle, and used to say: "Alas, so and so has lost his life and has missed the pleasures of this world!" Allah^{swt} revealed these verses clarifying that the Martyrs are not "dead" but definitely alive and fed by the Bounteous Lord. Of course, their lives are different and much better than ours.

"And ask those of our Messengers, whom we sent before you, 'Did We appoint any other god except the all-Affectionate, to be worshipped?' "
(Holy Qur'an 43:45)

This verse also proves that the prophets are alive because Allah^{swt} commands us to ask the Messengers about all matters. If they had passed away and mixed with the soil, surely we would not have been commanded to ask them about anything.

Evidence from *Ahadith*

Hazrat Abu Darda narrated that Allah's Messenger[S] said, 'Invoke many blessings on me on Friday for it is witnessed. The angels are present on it, and no one will invoke a blessing on me without his blessing being submitted to me till he stops.' I asked whether that applied also after his death, and he replied, 'Allah has prohibited the Earth from consuming the bodies of the prophets.' *(Ibn Majah 1,626)*

Thus, the Prophet Muhammad[S] has himself answered this question. He could have stated that prophets are dead and finished and there is no benefit in sending them anything. No. He said clearly they are alive by stating that their blessed bodies are as fresh as they were when they were buried – i.e. alive - but we don't understand.

Hazrat Anas bin Malik narrates Allah's Messenger[S] as saying: I happened to pass by the grave of Musa[A] on the occasion of the Night Journey near the red mound (and found him) standing and praying in his grave. *(Muslim 5,858)*

Clearly *Hazrat* Musa[A] was standing and praying - very much alive - in his grave. Thus we can say this is true for all prophets, after all, didn't they read prayer behind Prophet Muhammad[S] in *Masjid* Aqsa during *Isra*, before his blessed ascension to the heavens?

Abu Hurairah[R] narrated that the holy Prophet[S] said, 'When any one of you sends *salaam* to me Allah returns my soul to me and I return your *salaam*. *(Ahmad bin Hanbal 527, Abu Daood 2,036, Sahih from Hakim)*

Discussion

The Prophet Muhammad[S] left this world as a martyr from the poison given to him by a Jewess *(Bukhari 786)*. As he is a martyr and the greatest of Allah's creation then he is the greatest of the martyrs. The Holy Qur'an states that martyrs are alive and food is provided for them. The clear statement that they are alive should be enough. Allah[swt] even adds that they receive nourishment and clearly nourishment cannot be received by a dead person.

The beloved Prophet[S] said himself that even after his 'demise', we should continue to send blessings as they are still submitted to him. To say the Prophet[S] is dead is prohibited and to even think he is dead is prohibited.

12

Qs: You *sunnis* raise the status of the holy Prophet^S to a state that is too high when Allah states that he is a man "like you" *(Holy Qur'an 18:110)*

Answer: It is proven from Qur'an and *sunnah* that the holy Prophet^S is not a man 'like us' and the correct translation should be 'a man sent for our example'.

Evidence from the Holy Qur'an

> Say, "I am but a man for your example, receiving revelation from Allah that your Allah is one." *(Holy Qur'an 18:110 and 41:6)*

Looking more closely at these verse's we realise that it cannot and must not be said that the Prophet Muhammad^S is a man "like you" because he then goes onto say that he receives revelation from Allah^{swt}. Rather, "*basharum-mithlukum*" should be understood as "A man for your example".

> "Certainly you have in the Messenger of Allah an excellent example for anyone whose hope is in Allah and the last day, and who remembers Allah frequently." *(Holy Qur'an 33:21)*

Thus, the greatest of Allah's creation is sent as an example for everyone.

> "There is not an animal (that lives) on the earth, or a creature that flies on its wings but they are communities like you." *(Holy Qur'an 6:38)*

It is clear that no community of animals on earth is exactly like the community of mankind but we clearly understand that Allah^{swt} is referring to animal communities as being similar in example only - "*amthaalukum.*" They are not the same in nature or essence but as an example for us.

> They said: "You are only men like ourselves; and the beneficent Allah sends no sort of revelation: You do nothing but lie." *(HQ 36:15)*

Here Allah^{swt} is showing how previous community's used to insult and belittle Messengers who were sent to them by calling them "Men like us". Should we then do the same with our Messenger^S?

It is clear that in every verse of the Qur'an and in every *hadith* there is ample proof that the Prophet Muhammad[S] is not a man like any other ever created and cannot be viewed as such.

Evidence from *Ahadith*

Hazrat Anas[R] reported the Prophet Muhammad[S] said, "Do not practice *Al-Wisaal"* (This is fasting continuously without breaking ones fast in the evening or eating before the following dawn). The people said to the Prophet Muhammad[S], 'But you practice *Al-Wisaal*?' The Prophet Muhammad[S] replied, 'Are you like me? I am given food and drink (by Allah) during the night.' *(Bukhari 182)*

The beloved Prophet[S] clearly stated that he is not like anyone. Thus, he is the greatest of humans and the greatest of creation.

Abdullah ibn Mas'ud[R], said, "Verily, Allah looked at the hearts of the servants and He found that the heart of Muhammad[S], was the best among them; so He chose him for Himself and He sent him with His message; then, He looked at the hearts of His servants after Muhammad[S], and He found that the hearts of his companions were the best among them; thus, He made them into the ministers of His Prophet[S], fighting for the sake of his religion; and whatever the Muslims view as good is good in the sight of Allah, and whatever they view as evil is evil in the sight of Allah. " *(Ahmad, 3,589)*

Discussion

He is a Prophet, a Messenger, perspires musk, performs miracles, still prays for us today, is close to all believers, has *taqwa* beyond our imagination, possesses a huge amount of knowledge, is the beloved of Allah[swt], is the best of creation, is free from weakness, is innocent of mistakes and sin....etc. So how can anyone say he is 'like a normal human?' How can we say 'He is like us' (when we are sinful, weak, ignorant, forgetful etc.)?

There are many more *ahadith* with similar wording to the above showing clearly that the Prophet Muhammad[S] himself said that he is "NOT" like us, but much, much better than us. Should we then teach and understand something different to what Allah[swt] and the Prophet Muhammad[S] have taught us? The Prophet[S] is the greatest of all humans and is the greatest of creation.

13

Qs: Where is the evidence that you can celebrate the birth of the Prophet Muhammad[S]? (*Eid meelad un Nabi*)

Answer: Allah[swt] and His Messenger[S] and his noble companions celebrated it, so we are allowed to.

Evidence from Holy Qur'an

"Say in the blessing of Allah and His mercy, in that let them rejoice..."
(Holy Qur'an 10:58)

Allah Almighty allows celebration of the birth of Prophet Muhammad[S] in this verse. He declares that there should be happiness and rejoicing with the blessing of Allah and His mercy.

The Holy Qur'an refers to him as a mercy to the universe (21:107) and as a very great blessing (33:47), hence with his blessed arrival there should be celebration as a 'celebration' embodies both of these meanings – happiness and rejoicing. Or should we be upset and unhappy about his blessed birth?

Of course we can also say the Holy Qur'an is a great blessing as well. But, as the prophet Muhammad[S] is the embodiment of the Holy Qur'an, then on this level as well, he is a great blessing. So in honour of his arrival on this earth we should be happy and we should rejoice. We should remember Allah's blessing and mercy. Those who are not happy then they are going against the favour that Allah bestowed upon the believers. Another verse says:

"Publicise well the favours of your Lord." *(Holy Qur'an 93:11)*

The coming of the holy Prophet[S] is the greatest and exclusive of all divine favours *(HQ 3:146)*. So we should publicise it and celebrate it as did Allah[swt] in the Holy Qur'an (3:81) when he honoured him amongst all the prophets in a very special gathering.

Evidence from *Ahadith*

Narrated 'Ursa, 'Thuwaiba was the freed slave girl of Abu Lahb whom he had manumitted, and then she suckled the Prophet[S]. When Abu Lahb died, one of his relatives saw him in a dream in a very bad state and asked him, 'What have you encountered?' Abu Lahb said, "I have not found any rest since I left you, except that I have been given water to drink in this (the space between his thumb and other fingers) and that is because of my manumitting Thuwaiba. *(Bukhari 62:38)*

Abu Lahab freed Thuwaiba (his servant girl) on the joy at the birth of the holy Prophet[S]. The worst of the disbelievers is given some ease in his punishment from the finger he freed his servant girl Thuwaiba with. So even in the grave benefit is being received from celebrating his blessed birth (by a non-Muslim!). Then imagine the reward of a believer who celebrates and rejoices?

Abu Qatada Ansari[R] reported that Allah's Messenger[S] was asked about fasting on Monday, whereupon he said: 'It is the day when I was born and revelation was sent down to me. *(Muslim 2,603-2,606)*

The holy Prophet[S] fasted on his weekly birthday. He remembered the day of his birth and remembered it regularly. So we should also remember it regularly with a religious act as it's his *sunnah*.

Prophet Muhammad[S] went with Abu Darda[R] to the house of Amir Ansari[R] and found him to be talking about the events of the birth of Prophet Muhammad[S] to a gathering of his friends and children and was repeating 'this was the day' (i.e. 12th *Rabi-ul awwal*). The Prophet[S] stated, "O Amir[R] Allah has opened the doors of his mercy for you and the Angels are praying for your forgiveness. Whoever does this act of yours, he would also get the salvation like yours". *(Imam Suyuti[R] [4])* (A similar hadith is mentioned about *hazrat* Abdullah bin Abbas[R] in which the Prophet[S] also attended.)

Related by *hazrat* Anas[R] – 'The Prophet[S] performed his a*qeeqa* for himself after his prophet-hood' *(Baihaqqi 19,272 & 19,273 / 9:300)*

Subhanallah! Aqeeqa is celebrating ones birth and feeding others. Such is the *sunnah*. Or when we perform Aqeeqa for our children, should we do so with tears of sadness?

Discussion

Celebrating, announcing and showing happiness at the birth of Prophet Muhammad[S], is his own blessed *sunnah* the *sunnah* of his noble companions and the *sunnah* of Allah[swt].

27

14

Qs: **Prophet Muhammad^S became a prophet at the age of 40. Why do you say he was created as a Prophet?**

Answer: Prophet Muhammad^S was created a prophet and was born a prophet and announced his prophet-hood at the age of 40.

Evidence from Holy Qur'an

"And remember when we took the pledge from the Prophets <u>and from you</u>, and from Nuh and Ibrahim and Musa and Isa son of Maryam and we took from them a firm covenant." *(Holy Qur'an 33:7)*.

"Remember when we took the covenant from (all) the prophets..." *(Holy Qur'an 3:81)*

These clearly show the holy Prophet^S and other prophets came to existence before anyone was born. The Holy Qur'an testifies to this fact and specifically mentions that we took pledge from 'you' referring to the holy Messenger^S.

"And we did not send you, but as mercy for all the worlds." *(Holy Qur'an 21:107)*

For one to be sent he has to have existed somewhere. The holy Prophet^S awaited his mission as a final prophet and the right time to undertake it. For the holy prophet says in the Holy Qur'an:

"This I have been commanded; and I am the first of the Muslims" *(Holy Qur'an 6:163)*

In many verses in the Holy Qur'an the position of the prophet of Allah is referred to as the first Muslim, regardless of being the last of all prophets who are all Muslims. So this shows us that the holy prophet's creation was before anyone else and his remembrance was way before creation.

The blessed Prophet^S came to fulfil his mission as mercy to the entire universe, a Warner, giver of glad tidings, witness etc, but his prophet hood was already confirmed and remains in force.

Evidence from *Ahadith*

Sayyidina Jabir bin Abdullah narrates, 'I said, 'O Messenger of Allah. May my mother and father be sacrificed for you. Please inform me of the first thing Allah almighty created'. He said 'O Jabir, indeed Allah first created the light of your prophet from his light. Then the light began to go around wherever Allah willed. At that time there was no divine tablet, no divine pen, no paradise, nor hell fire, no angel, nor heavens, no sun, no moon, nor jinn, nor human'. *(Sharh az zurqani 1:89)*

Sayyidina Abu Huraira[R] said that the companions asked the prophet[S]: O Messenger of Allah, when did prophet hood become compulsory upon you? Our beloved Prophet[S] said: 'At the time when Adam was between body and soul'. *(Tirmithi: 3,852)*

Abu Hurairah related that the holy Prophet[S] said, 'I was the first prophet to be created and the last to be sent.' And in another narration, 'the first person to be created'. *(Ibn Abi Shayba Musannaf 8:131) [5]*

Clearly the Prophet Muhammad[S] is the first of creation and he was created as a Prophet.

Hazrat Jabir bin Samura[R] reported Allah's Messenger[S] said: I recognise the stone in Mecca which used to pay me salutations before my announcement as a Prophet and I recognise it even now. *(Muslim 5,654).*

If stones recognised the prophet-hood before announcement and acknowledged by the Prophet[S] himself, then why would anyone question this?

Discussion

If the notion is entertained that Prophet Muhammad[S] is not created as such, then are we saying that Allah has not planned for his creation nor for our guidance? This is nonsense. Allah[swt] is the best of planners *(HQ 3:54 &13:42).*

It is clear that the holy Prophet[S] is the first of Allah's creation and is the best of Allah's creation. He is created as a Prophet, born as a Prophet, remains a Prophet and announced his mission at the age of 40. To deny otherwise is to deny Qur'an and *ahadith.*

15

Qs: Why do you kiss your thumbs when the name of Prophet Muhammad[S] is mentioned?

Answer: To kiss ones thumbs has been approved and encouraged by Prophet Muhammad[S] and practised by his noble companions[R].

Evidence from Holy Qur'an

"When you proclaim your call to prayer..." *(Holy Qur'an 5:58)*

In his commentary of this verse, the great *Mufassir hazrat* Isma'eel Haqqi[R] states in his *tafseer, Roohul Bayaan* that it has been agreed by *Muhadditheen* that kissing the nails of the thumbs and the *shahaadah* finger should be acted upon as it inclines people towards good deeds and instils fear within them.

Evidence from *Ahadith*

Whenever he (Abu Bakr[R]) heard the *Mu-athin* say, 'I bear witness that Muhammad[S] is the Messenger of Allah', he would repeat this phrase (as is the *sunnah*) and would kiss the tip of the index fingers (or thumbs) and wipe his eyes. The Prophet[S] said, 'Whosoever does what my friend (i.e. Abu Bakr) did, my intercession will become essential for him.' (*Maqaasid-e-Hasana 1,021*)

It is clear that *hazrat* Abu Bakr[R] kissed his thumbs on the mention of the beloved Prophet[S] name and that the Prophet[S] not just approved but said that he will ensure he would specially intercede for such a person.

Once, the Holy Prophet[S] entered the *Masjid* and sat down near a pillar. *Hazrat* Abu Bakr Siddiq[R] was seated beside him. *Hazrat* Bilal[R] then stood up and commenced with the *Athaan*. When he said: '*Ash hadu Anna Muhammadur Rasoolullah'*, *hazrat* Abu Bakr Siddiq[R] placed both the thumb nails on to his eyes and said '*Qurratu 'Aini bika Ya Rasoolallah[S].*' (*Yaa Rasoolallah[S]*, you are the coolness of my eyes). When *hazrat* Bilal[R] completed the *Athaan*, the holy Prophet[S] said, "O Abu Bakr, whosoever does like you have done, Almighty Allah will forgive all his sins." (*Tafseer Roohul Bayaan for HQ 5:58, & al Daylami*)

"That person, who when hearing my name in *athaan*, kisses his thumb nails and turns it over his eyes, he shall never go blind." (*Tafseer Roohul Bayaan for HQ 5:58*)

The Holy Prophet[S] said, 'Whosoever has touched the name Muhammad[S] with his hands, then kissed his hand with his lips and rubbed it on his eyes, then he will see Allah[swt] just as the righteous ones see and my intercession will be close to him even though he is a sinner.' (*An Nawafi ul Atriyaa p51*)

'The Noble Messenger[S] is reported to have said, 'On the day of resurrection, I shall search for the person who used to place his thumbs on his eyes when hearing my name during the *Athan*. I shall lead him into *Jannah*.' (*Salaate-Mas'oodi 23.1 - Vol. 2, Chapter 20 & Bahrur-raaiq Ramili vol 1*)

None of these *ahadith* are fabricated or made up (i.e. *Maudu'*) but some can be argued to be 'weak' with regards hadith classification. In terms of *Shari'ah*, a weak *hadith* does not mean that it is made up or should be rejected, only that such actions mentioned are considered as *fadaail a'maal* (extra actions of devotion). We dont't use such *ahadith* to make actions *fard* (compulsory) or *waajib* (compulsory via presumption) unless supported by stronger *ahadith*. At the very least scholars have indicated that such an act is permissible and even *mustahab* – i.e. it will be rewarded if done.

Discussion

The practice of kissing ones thumbs and placing them on one's eyes is known as *Taqbeelul Ibhaamain* and has been confirmed in many books including *kanzul-'ibaad, Qohistani and in fataawa soofia*. One of the greatest ways to show love is to follow his *sunnah*, but this specific action shows a personal affection and deep love of the Prophet[S].

It is clear that Prophet Muhammad[S] has said this and that true devotees of him and ones who love him will happily show love in this way as *hazrat* Abu Bakr[R]. This is thus an act of devotion that only the truly devoted will give emphasis to.

31

16

Qs: **Prove that the Prophet Muhammad^S knows about the unseen ('Ilm-e-Ghayb)**

Answer: Allah^{swt} revealed knowledge of the Unseen to the Prophet^S and he clearly knows of the unseen.

Evidence from Holy Qur'an

"He (Allah) is the Knower of the Unseen, and He does not disclose the unseen to anyone, except the Messenger whom He is pleased with."
(Holy Qur'an 72:26)

This verse informs believers that Allah^{swt} has knowledge of all the unseen (that which is hidden from normal view) and that he has disclosed this to His Messenger Muhammad^S. So clearly, our beloved Prophet^S has knowledge of the unseen.

"And he (Allah) revealed to his servant (Muhammad) whatever he revealed" *(Holy Qur'an 53:10)*

Whatever has been concealed in the ambiguity of the verse has not been established or elaborated upon. It clearly shows that the branches of knowledge and wisdom that were bestowed upon the holy Prophet^S on the night of ascension is beyond our comprehension and understanding. Allah has not divulged how much knowledge, wisdom and blessing He has bestowed.

Evidence from *Ahadith*

The Prophet^S stated, 'I have seen my Lord, He put His hand upon my back, after which everything appeared before me and I recognized everything.' *(Ahmad v5 page 243 & Tirmithi 3,235).* (In one version in Tabarani: 'So I acquired knowledge of the truth of everything and I observed it as well.')

Subhanallah! A direct transfer of knowledge from the Almighty to the blessed heart of the greatest of creation via his blessed seal of prophet-hood. No-one can now be in any doubt as to the fact that he knows everything. There are different levels of knowledge which we do not know about but the Prophet^S does know.

Hazrat Huzaifa narrates: the holy Prophet[S] delivered a speech in front of us where he left nothing but mentioned everything that will happen till the hour. Some of us remembered and some forgot. I used to see events taking place but I had forgotten about them. Then I would recognize such events as a man recognizes another man who has been absent and then sees and recognizes him. *(Bukhari 601)*

How else did Prophet Muhammad[S] describe the future unless he had knowledge of the unseen?

Once the people started asking Allah's Apostle questions ... and he ascended the pulpit and said, 'I will answer whatever questions you may ask me today.'.... Then there was a man who used to quarrel with the people about his father. He said, "O Allah's Apostle, who is my father?" The Prophet[S] replied, "Your father is Hudhaifa." ... Allah's Apostle said, 'I have never seen a day like today in its good and its evil for Paradise and the Hell Fire were displayed in front of me, till I saw them just beyond this wall.' *(Bukhari 373)*

The Prophet Muhammad[S] did not wait for revelation to explain who the person's father was – he already knew as he had knowledge of the unseen – plus he could see paradise and hell as easily as we see what is in front of us.

Hazrat Usamah[R] narrates that the holy Prophet[S] climbed to a fort of Madinah and said, "Do you see what I see? Certainly I observe the trials pouring upon your houses like drops of rain". *(Bukhari 3,507)*.

His vast knowledge includes people's trials which are clear for him to see! How can anyone see such a thing? Well, the Prophet[S] can! Before the battle of Badr the Prophet Muhammad[S] declared, 'This is the place of slaughter of so and so,' placing his hand on the ground. They all died at the place indicated, again proving his vast knowledge of the unseen. *(Muslim 1,779 & Abu Daood 2,071)*

Discussion

Some try to belittle the knowledge of the Prophet[S] in contrast to how Allah has elevated his status. It is crystal clear from the above evidences that Allah has granted knowledge of unseen to the holy Prophet[S] and as far as we are concerned the degree of this vision and knowledge is beyond our estimation and imagination.

17

Qs: You claim that the Prophet Muhammad[S] has a huge amount of knowledge – where is the proof?

Answer: The holy Prophet[S] has been granted so much knowledge that our minds can't comprehend.

Evidence from Holy Qur'an

"And we gave you the knowledge (O Muhammad) what you did not know and Allah's favour is immense upon you." *(Holy Qur'an 4:113)*

The verse shows us that Allah[swt] taught the holy Prophet[S] the laws of *shari'ah* and affairs of religion and <u>everything that he did not know</u>. Thus, He informed of all the secrets and made him aware of their truths and granted him all knowledge of what was, what is and what will be. Therefore, there is nothing he doesn't know as far as we are concerned, because this verse explains that if he didn't know it – he knows it now.

"And we revealed to you the Qur'an that is an exposition (account) of everything" *(Holy Qur'an 16:89)*

The verse leaves us to conclude that every minor and major thing that is recorded in the Qur'an Allah has taught it to the holy prophet. So the question then follows is: what exactly has Allah[swt] revealed to Prophet Muhammad[S]. The answer follows: "...an <u>explanation of all things</u>". So the Holy Qur'an contains an explanation of everything and it has been revealed to him. Therefore the holy Prophet[S] has the <u>knowledge of all things.</u> Just as he says *Ar-Rahman* (the merciful) taught his beloved the Holy Qur'an *(Holy Qur'an 81:1-2)*.

Evidence from *Ahadith*

Hazrat Umar[R] narrates: One day the Prophet[S] stood up amongst us for a long period and informed us about the beginning of creation (and talked about everything in detail) till he mentioned how the people of paradise will enter their places and how the people of hell will enter their places. Some remembered what he had said, and some forgot it.
(Bukhari: 414)

Clearly, he had that much knowledge that he stood in front of people and informed them of the incidents and events that are to take place in the future all the way up to the entry into paradise and hell. How then can anyone then dispute that the Prophet Muhammad[S] has not been endowed with a huge amount of knowledge by his Lord. He did not wait for revelation, he already knew.

Hazrat Ibne 'Abbas[R] narrated the holy Prophet[S] said: '...Tonight my blessed Lord came to me in the best appearance...Then I saw Him (Allah) put his palm between my shoulder blades till I felt the coolness of his hand in my chest. Then I knew what is in the heavens and earth...' *(Tirmithi: 3,244 & Ahmad 5:243 and 22,170 [6]).*

Subhanallah! Allah wanted to give him so much knowledge that rather than reveal it, he transferred it spiritually and directly, such that everything became recognisable to his blessed heart. Even the great Imam Ahmad bin Hambal[R] agrees as he quotes this amazing *hadith*. How lucky we are to gain an insight into the close and beautiful relationship between Allah[swt] and Prophet Muhammad[S].

Abu Dharr[R] narrates, 'When the Messenger[S] of Allah left us, there was not a bird that flies in the sky but that he had given us some knowledge about it.' *(Ahmad 5:153, Tabarani 1,647)*

Such is the depth and breadth of the knowledge of the Prophet[S] such that his noble companions[R] were astounded and in awe. The fact that he mentioned birds shows he is versed in all types of knowledge. There is a *hadith* that some people quote (*Muslim 2,362*) regarding cross-pollination of crops and they use this to try and prove that the Prophet[S] did not have knowledge of this. However, (as discussed in Appendix 1) this has been miss-reported by one of the narrators by his own admission so should not be relied upon.

Discussion

We are informed that Allah[swt] taught His Messenger[S] that which was unknown to him - from the knowledge of Islamic jurisprudence to secrets of the entire creation and beyond. Thus according to our limited intellect, his knowledge is correct, vast and without any human limit.

18

Qs: Prove that the Prophet^S was the first to be created?

Answer: The light (*noor*) and essence of Prophet
Muhammad^S, was the first creation of Allah
Almighty.

Evidence from Holy Qur'an

"He (Allah) has no partner an with this I have been commanded, <u>and I am
the first Muslim</u>" *(Holy Qur'an 6:163)*

In many verses in the holy Qur'an the position of the prophet of
Allah is referred to as the first Muslim, regardless of being the last
of all prophets who are all Muslims. So this shows us that the holy
Prophet's creation was way back and his remembrance was way
before creation.

"Indeed from Allah came a light and a clear book" *(Holy Qur'an 5:15)*

Mufassiroon agree that this light is our beloved Prophet
Muhammad^S. In *Roohul Bayaan*, a hadith related to this verse is
quoted as:

'I am the father of the souls and I am from the light of Allah". *(Roohul
Bayaan on HQ 5:15)*

This, hadith also confirms that he is the first creation as a 'father'
comes before his children. While *hazrat* Adam^A is the bodily father
of us all, the spiritual father of our souls is our beloved prophet
Muhammad^S. (Please see Appendix 1 for more information.)

Evidence from *Ahadith*

Abu Huraira^R related that the holy Prophet^S said, 'I was the first
prophet to be created and the last to be sent'. And in another narration,
'the first person to be created'. *(Ibn Abi Shayba Musannaf, 8:131) [7]*

This *hadith* clearly states that the first of creation was our beloved
Prophet Muhammad^S as does the following *hadith*:

Sayyidina Jabir bin Abdullah^R narrates, 'I said: 'O messenger of Allah,
may my mother and father be sacrificed for you. Please inform me of

the first thing Allah almighty created.' He said 'O Jabir. Certainly before anything else, Allah created the light of your prophet from His light. Then the light began to go around wherever Allah willed. At that time there was no divine tablet, no divine pen, no paradise, no hell fire, no angel, no heavens, no sun, no moon, nor jinn, nor human....'
(Sharh az Zurqani 1:89)

Thus, the Prophet[S] himself has mentioned that his blessed light was created from the blessed light of Allah[swt]. It shows how pure and amazing his creation was and that he was the first to have been created.

Abu Hurairah[R] narrates that the Messenger[S] of Allah said: 'When Allah created Adam[A] He informed him of his descendants, at this Adam[A] saw superiority of some over others, then he saw me towards the end in form of an illuminating light (*noor*) he (Adam[A]) said: O my Lord who is this? The Lord replied: This is your son Ahmed who is the first and the last and he will be first to intercede (on the Day of Judgment). *(Baihaqqi in Dalail an Nabuwwah: Vol 5, Page 483)*

Again, as clearly stated, the beloved Prophet Muhammad[S] is the first to have been created and that his creation was light or *noor*. The *ahadith* are totally clear *mashaAllah*.

Discussion

The light (*noor*) of the holy Prophet[S] was the first of Allah's creation and also the reason of all creation as the above evidences clearly states. Allah chose him over his creation and declared his rank before the beginning of creation as evidence from the verse of the Qur'an.

There is a *hadith* that people quote regarding the 'pen' being the first to have been created [8]. However, the *hadith* states that Allah[swt] instructed the pen to write what will happen and what had already happened. The pen could not have been first if it is ordered to write what had already happened.

The special essence of Prophet Muhammad[S] is light and this blessed light is the very first of Allah's creation and on this there is no doubt. In any case, surely Allah[swt] would create His most beloved first? Yes He did so we shouldn't deny it.

37

19

Qs: **The parents of the holy Prophet^S passed away before they could accept him as a Prophet how can you say that they are Muslims?**

Answer: The parents of the holy Prophet^S are believers and they died on *imaan* (belief)

Evidence from Qur'an

"You were transmitted from those who do *sajdah*." *(HQ 26:219)*

The greatest commentator and scholar of all times *hazrat* Abdullah ibn Abbas^R commenting on the word *taqallubaka* in this verse and he said it refers to the holy prophet's soul being transmitted from one messenger & father through to the next until he manifested himself in this *ummah*. He also reported to have said, 'Allah's Messenger^S moved through pure loins of one father to the next until he manifested himself.' *(Masalikul hunafa nr40)*. In *Tafseer Saavi* the holy Prophet^S passed from pure loins of *hazrat* Adam^A and *hazrat* Hawwa^A (Eve) until he reached the beloved parents of the holy Prophet^S. Thus, according to the Holy Qur'an, the parents of Prophet Muhammad^S are Muslims.

Evidence from *Ahadith*

The holy Prophet^S is reported to have said when Allah created creation and he made me the best of creation and the best of the two (man and Jinn). Then he created tribes and chose me from the best of the tribes and he created families and chose me from best of the families. Therefore, I am the best of you by virtue of self and family. *(Tirmithi 3,627 & 3,628)*

MashaAllah, clearly, he is the best of creation and from the best tribe and from the best parents (i.e. families). How can the best of creation come from any other than Muslim parents?

Abu Naeem narrated in Al-Dalael from Ibn Abbas^R that he said that the messenger of Allah said: 'My fathers' never met on adultery, Allah was transferring me from the good loins to the pure wombs with purity and elegance within both branches (mother's side and father's side). I am in the best one (from both).' *(Tafseer Dur al-Manthur, surah 9:128)*

As narrated by Abu Hurairah[R], 'I have been sent in the best of all generations of Adam's offspring since their creation.' *(Bukhari 757)*

Hazrat Ayesha[R] said the holy Prophet[S] once asked *Hazrat Jibraeel*[A] about the virtue of his family. He replied, 'I travelled all the corners of the world from east to west but did not find anyone nobler than you nor did I find any family nobler than *banu hashim.'* *(Mishkaat 511)*

Narrated *hazrat* Ayesha[R] that the Prophet[S] one day came by *Hujun* in Makkah and he was sad. He stayed there for some time and then he returned very happy. He said to Ayesha[R], "I asked Allah[swt] to revive my mother. She accepted me and believed in me and then Allah took her back." *(Mawahib Lidunya vol 2 p240 [9])*

Narrated *hazrat* Ayesha[R] 'The parents of the Prophet[S] were brought back to life until they believed in him.' *(Mawahib Lidunya vol 2 p240)*

Discussion

If his honourable mother was a disbeliever, why was permission given to visit her grave when it says in the Holy Qur'an (9:84) not to visit the graves of disbelievers? Thus – she is a believer. As to the question of forgiveness he did not ask for her forgiveness because she was not a sinner. A sinner or disbeliever is one upon whom a set of divine laws has reached and who intentionally violates it. A set of pure Divine Laws did not reach the parents of the Prophet[S], yet they believed in one God and did not commit sins.

People try and use a *hadith* in Muslim (nr 398) to show that the Prophets father is in Hell fire, but the Arabic used means uncle in this case, not father. The honourable father of our beloved Prophet[S] is called 'Abdullah' which means 'slave and worshipper of Allah' and his honourable mother, Amina[R], which means 'one with faith'. Thus their names alone prove their *Iman* (faith).

The verse of the Qur'an and *ahadith* are clear – all forefathers of Prophet Muhammad[S], are Muslims. *Hazrat* Abdullah[R] and *hazrat* Amina[R] took *shahaadah* at the blessed hand of the holy Prophet[S] in a special ceremony. To say otherwise is against Holy Qur'an, against *ahadith* and against reality. Also, such lies would certainly hurt our beloved Prophet[S].

20

Qs: **The Qur'an and _hadith_ that show that the holy Prophet^S made mistakes, why do you say he is free from weakness?**

Answer: This is incorrect. The Qur'an and _hadith_ show that the beloved Prophet^S is sinless, totally free from misguidance and totally free from bodily or spiritual weakness.

Evidence from Holy Qur'an

"And verily, you (Muhammad^S) stand on an exalted character."
(Holy Qur'an 68:4)

The Qur'an clearly teaches that the holy Prophet^S is the most perfect of Allah's creation. For this when the mother of believers _Sayyidina Ayesha^R_ was asked about the character of the messenger of Allah she answered that he was the embodiment (the example) of a living Qur'an _(Muslim 746)_.

"Muhammad is the Messenger of Allah..." _(Holy Qur'an 48:29)_

Transgression, weakness and prophet-hood cannot be combined. The prophet Muhammad^S is the best of Allah creation. If he could make a mistake then this means Allah having misguided him!? Thus our Prophet^S <u>cannot sin or make a mistake</u>.

"Whoever obeys the messenger, indeed he has indeed obeyed Allah."
(Holy Qur'an 4:80)

Allah shows the perfection of Prophet Muhammad^S in that following him, means following Allah. Thus, as Allah does not make mistakes, neither can the beloved Prophet^S. The following and obedience of the Messenger^S would be impossible if he was a sinner or made mistakes.

"Indeed you have in the Messenger of Allah a beautiful example..."
(Holy Qur'an 33:21)

He is a beautiful example for us which doesn't mean misguided or liable to make mistakes. It means perfection. If Allah^{swt} mentions that someone made a 'mistake', then that is for Allah to say, not us as He is the guide of the Prophets. It is not for sinners like us to comment or to try and judge the greatest of His creation.

Evidence from *Ahadith*

Abdullah ibn Mas'ud[R], said, "Verily, Allah looked at the hearts of the servants and He found that the heart of Muhammad, was the best among them; so He chose him for Himself and He sent him with His message. *(Musnad Ahmad 3,589)*

Having the best of hearts simply means he is the best of his creation in every way.

Anas b. Malik[R] reported that Allah's Apostle used to come to our house and there was perspiration upon his body. My mother brought a bottle and began to pour the sweat into it. When Allah's Apostle got up he said: *Umm Sulaimi*[R], what is this that you are doing? She said, 'That is your perspiration which we mix in our perfume and it becomes the most fragrant and best of all perfumes.' *(Muslim 5,761)*

Sayyidina Malik bin Sunan[R], the father of *Sayyidina Abu Saeed Khudri*[R], began to suck out the blood from the wound of the Holy Prophet[S] (during *Uhud*) and it began to look white. The *Sahaba* asked him to spit it out. He refused to do so and said, 'I swear by Allah that I will never spit this blood out of my mouth.' He then swallowed the blessed blood of the Holy Prophet[S], who said, 'Whoever of you wishes to see a *Jannati* (man of paradise), you should look at him (*Hazrat* Malik bin Sunaan*[R])*'. *(Shifa Shareef, Madarijun Nubuwat, hayat sahaba).*

Subhanallah! So perfect is he that his blessed perspiration is sweeter than perfume and by swallowing his blessed blood, we are saved from *Jahannam!*

Discussion

All the Prophets[A] are free from sins and we are in no position to criticise them. The guidance of Prophet Muhammad[S] comes directly from Allah[swt]. We must accept his infallibility as he has reached perfection. If our prophets 'misguided us' then it will not be just of the Almighty to punish us. The purity and perfection of the holy Prophet[S] was not restricted to his heart and soul, but it extended to his beloved body, his character, his knowledge, his example, his *taqwa* and all aspects about him - which only shows he is above perfection. (Please also see Appendix 1.)

21   Qs: Isn't asking the dead for help *Shirk*?

Answer: No. We can ask directly from the pious in their graves (believing they help with the permission of Allah^{swt}) and/or we can make *du'a* obtaining blessing from the grave (see chapter 25).

Evidence from Holy Qur'an

"And, if when they wronged themselves, they had come to you (O Prophet) and asked forgiveness of Allah and the Messenger had asked forgiveness for them, they would have found Allah accepting of repentance and Merciful" *(Holy Qur'an 4:64)*

An Arab came to the grave of Prophet Muhammad^S and said, 'I repent from my sins through you and ask for forgiveness; I would give my life for you'. Afterwards, the holy Prophet^S came in the dream of *hazrat* Utba'^R saying, 'tell him Allah has forgiven his sins.' (*Tafsir* Ibne Kathir of this verse). In another version, a voice came from the grave of the Prophet^S saying, 'Allah has forgiven your sins', (*Tafsir* Qurtabi under this verse).

"So ask the people of *thikr* (remembrance) if you do not know" *(Holy Qur'an 16:43)*

Are not all the prophets in the above category and also the noble companions^R? So, Allah^{swt} is requiring that we ask them for help. The fact they are in *barzakh* is irrelevant as the Holy Qur'an is timeless. So asking Allah^{swt} through someone who is pious and deceased is permissible. Didn't Musa^A suggest that the 50 prayers given by Allah^{swt} to Prophet Muhammad^S be reduced? Musa^A was a person of the grave at the time and Allah^{swt} requires that <u>all</u> the prophets in *barzakh* help Prophet Muhammad^S from their graves:

"..You must believe in him and <u>you must help him</u>.." *(HQ 3:81)*

Evidence from *Ahadith*

"The people of Medina were in the grip of a severe famine. They complained to 'Ayesha^R (about their terrible condition). She told them

to go to the grave of the holy Prophet[S] and to open a window in the direction of the sky so that there is no curtain between the sky and the grave. The narrator says they did so. Then it started raining heavily; even the lush green grass sprang up (everywhere) and the camels had grown so fat (it seemed) they would burst out due to the over piling of blubber. So the year was named as the year of greenery and plenty.
(Mishkaat 5,950, Daarimi 43:93)

The *hadith* above highlights that one is able to seek help from the Prophet[S] who is at the time of this *hadith* deceased. *Sayyidina* 'Ayesha[R] herself is condoning and instructing people to go and seek assistance from a deceased person – proving that assistance can be sought from someone pious whom is deceased.

There is another tradition where someone came to the grave of the Prophet[S] in the time of drought to ask for help. He then saw the Prophet[S] in a dream who instructed him to go to *hazrat* 'Umar[R], say salam and to inform him rain was coming. *(Baihaqqi – Dalail)*.

Sinan[R] narrates from his father, 'I swear by Allah that I placed Thabit in his grave and I was with Humaid al Tawil or somebody else. When we had completed the levelling of the soil a brick fell down and Thabit became visible praying in his grave. I said to my companion, 'Have you not seen?' He replied, 'Keep silent.' We re-levelled the earth then asked his daughter, 'What was the practise of your father?' ..... She replied, 'For 50 years he prayed all night and at the time of *suhur* he would say, 'O Allah! If you grant anyone from your creation prayers in his grave, let him be me. Allah accepted his *du'a.'* *(Al-Hilyah 2:219)*

The *hadith* above (and the *hadith* of Musa[A] praying in his grave *Muslim 5,858)*, show that the pious are alive in their graves, praying and making *du'a*.

Discussion

With the relevant proofs from the Qur'an and *sunnah* it is evident that not only is asking help from the dead not *shirk*, it is in fact a highly commendable action encouraged by Allah[swt], the holy Prophet[S] and his followers. The pious dead are not helpless, but they are extremely helpful. Thus the pious dead can help the living.

22

Qs: **Why should we read Qur'an or give *sadaqah* for those who have passed away when it can't reach them?**

Answer: We read Qur'an or give *sadaqa* to send blessings to the deceased and seek Allah's forgiveness for them - and it <u>does</u> reach them – according to the Qur'an and *sunnah*.

Evidence from Holy Qur'an

"And we reveal from the Qur'an that which is healing and mercy upon the believers" *(Holy Qur'an 17:82)*

Verily the Qur'an is a healing and mercy to those who believe whether dead or alive. Through its recitation Allah's countless blessings can be attained and transferred - this is known as *esaal-e-thawab'*. We are also allowed to make du'a for the dead:

'Our Lord, forgive us and forgive our Muslim brothers who have come before us with *Iman. (Holy Qur'an 59:10)*

If praying for the deceased was not allowed Allah would not have instructed us to ask for forgiveness for those passed away.

Evidence from *Ahadith*

Ata' ibn Abi Rabah said: I heard Ibn `Umar say: I heard the Holy Prophet[S] say, 'When one of you dies do not wait, but make haste and take him to his grave, and let someone read at his head the opening of *Surah Baqarah*, and at his feet its closure when he lies in the grave.' *(Mishkaat 1,717, Baihaqqi 7,068 ch 137 5:404)*

Clearly, the prophet Muhammad[S], instructed one of his companions to recite Qur'an for the deceased. In this case <u>at his grave</u> so that there could be no doubt or argument that this action is his *sunnah* and it was for benefit of the deceased. This is further confirmed by the following *hadith*:

The holy Prophet[S] said, 'Recite *surah yaseen* over your dead'. *(Abu Daood 3,115)*

Why instruct this if the blessing cannot reach the dead? The fact is, it does reach them and to prove that this blessing can be transferred from the living, the following *ahadith* are clear:

Hazrat Anas[R] narrated, 'The holy Prophet[S] made du'a on the grave of a lady after she was buried.' *(Baihaqqi 7,010)*

Narrated by *hazrat* Anas[R], 'The Prophet[S] passed by a grave and made *du'a* and said, 'verily these graves are filled with darkness and Allah enlightens them with prayers.' *(Baihaqqi 7,011)*

The Prophet[S] himself made *du'a* for their enlightenment, so it is his *sunnah* to make *du'a* for the dead and this does benefit them.

Abu Hurairah[R] reported that the Prophet[S] said, 'When a person dies all his good deeds cease except for three: (1) continuous act of charity, (2) beneficial knowledge (that he taught or spread when he was alive) and (3) a righteous son who prays for him.' *(Tirmithi 1,376)*

Thus blessing can continuously be received even when one is in the grave from actions one has performed when alive and by the *du'a* (prayers) of others. This is again confirmed in the following *hadith*:

It was narrated that Ibn 'Abbas[R] said that Allah's Messenger[S] passed by two graves and said, 'They are being punished, but they are not being punished for anything that was difficult to avoid. One of them used to spread malicious gossip (*nameemah*), and the other used not to take precautions to avoid getting urine on himself when he urinated.' Then he called for a green branch (with leaves), which he split in two and planted a piece on each grave, and said, 'May their torment be reduced so long as these do not dry out.' *(Bukhari 213, Muslim 292)*

If a leaf can benefit a dead person then a Muslim reading Qur'an can also provide benefit, or is the leaf greater than the Holy Qur'an?

Discussion

Clearly reading Qur'an for the dead and asking Allah to send blessings is the *sunnah* of the Prophet Muhammad[S] and his noble companions[R]. Dead people can receive blessings from those of us who are living. *Salatul janaazah* itself is prayer for the dead, so there should be no objection. Or do we not wish for our *janazah* to be read? Clearly, the living can benefit the dead.

23

Qs: How can you build tombs over the graves of the prophets and others when Allah has forbidden this?

Answer: It is totally permissible to build structures over the graves of prophets and saints with the intention of a honouring them to attain blessings and *du'a*.

Evidence from Holy Qur'an

"Let us surely build a place of worship over them." *(HQ 18:21)*

After the advent of the companions of the cave who were great servants of Allah^swt there was a dispute between the believers and the disbelievers with regard to building a monument around them. Those who prevailed were the true believers who built over them a place of worship at the entrance of the cave.   *(Tafseer al Jalalyn, Volume No.1, Page No. 389).*

Almighty Allah informs us about this decision and where the 'people of the cave' slept for many years became a place of prostration to Allah - a place of worship. Thus to build structures of worship in honour of a place and to honour people is totally permissible.

"Appoint for yourselves a place of prayer on standing on the place of Ibrahim." *(Holy Qur'an 2:125)*

The place of Ibrahim^A generally known as *maqaame-Ibrahim* is a construction done by *hazrat* Ibrahim^A and *hazrat* Isma'eel^A. As *hazrat* Isma'eel^A would pass the bricks to his father, the very place the father was standing became sanctified and Allah^swt gave an order for us to worship at that very place and named it a place of prostration. Thus to worship Allah in a place touched by great people is totally permissible. In this case, the blessed foot of Ibrahim^A touching the ground makes everyone wish to pray there. So important it is – that Allah^swt made a special mention of it in His Holy Book and instructed prayer at that place in his honour.

Evidence from *Ahadith*

Narrated by Ibn Umar[R] from the holy Prophet[S] who said, 'In the Mosque of al-Khayf there are graves of 70 Prophets (together*). (Majma Zawaid Volume No.3 chapter on Masjid al Khayf, Hadith :5769)*

Thus, a place worship has been constructed over graves of numerous prophets and the Prophet Muhammad[S] has approved of this.

Narrated 'Amr bin Maimun Al-Audi: I saw 'Umar bin Al-Khattab (when he was stabbed) saying, "O 'Abdullah bin 'Umar! Go to the mother of the believers Aisha and say, 'Umar bin Al-Khattab[R] sends his greetings to you,' and request her to allow me to be buried with my companions." (So, Ibn 'Umar conveyed the message to 'Aisha) She said, "I had the idea of having this place for myself but today I prefer him ('Umar) to myself (and allow him to be buried there)." When 'Abdullah bin 'Umar returned, 'Umar asked him, "What (news) do you have?" He replied, "O chief of the believers! She has allowed you (to be buried there)." On that 'Umar said, "Nothing was more important to me than to be buried in that (sacred) place. So, when I expire, carry me there and pay my greetings to her ('Aisha)...' *(Bukhari 475)*

Thus, Hazrat 'Umar[R] desired to be buried in a grave, next to Prophet[S] and *hazrat* Abu Bakr[R] in the Mosque of the Prophet[S]. If it was not allowed, he would have not permitted himself or *hazrat* Abu Bakr[R] to be buried there. Indeed, Hazrat Abu Bakr[R] would not have allowed himself to be buried there and this blessed tomb (*mizaar*) is visited by almost every Muslim born.

Discussion

A tomb is a room built around the grave. The very place where the holy Prophet[S] is buried and none of the companions took it as an innovation but rather a place of attaining blessings and spirituality.

Almighty Allah ordered believers to pray at that very place where his friend and a prophet *hazrat* Ibrahim[A] stepped on. Allah[swt] approved the practise of those believers who built a Masjid over the companions of the cave. This shows us we can build structures over these blessed and sanctified places where prophets and saints are buried.

24

Qs: **Why do the 40 day *khatams* (Qur'an reading) for the dead and then annual ones when there is no evidence.**

Answer: It is a confirmed *sunnah* to pass on reward to the dead on days 3, 7 & 40 and after 6 & 12 months.

Evidence from Holy Qur'an

When it comes to fixing of dates the Almighty says in the holy Qur'an:

> "And remind them of the days of Allah" *(Holy Qur'an 14:5).*

Allah[swt] clearly indicates that there are special days associated with His majesty. The Holy Qur'an indicates that the day of birth, death and resurrection are special such as for Prophet *Yahya*[A]:

> "Peace be upon him the day he was born, the day he will die and the day he will be raised." *(Holy Qur'an 19:15)*

Thus the days of birth (birth-day), day of death (death-day) and day of resurrection are significant in the eyes of Allah[swt] so they should be significant in our eyes as well.

Evidence from *Ahadith*

In the book *Anwar-e-Satiah* (p.145) and *Hashiyah Khazanatur Riwayaat* it is written that the Holy Prophet[S] offered *Sadaqa* on the third, seventh and fortieth day of the *Wafaat* (*Shahaadah*) of Sayyidina Amir Hamzah[R] and repeated the same at every sixth months and at the end of the year. Thus it is *sunnah* to offer some gift to the deceased (in the above case, *sadaqa*) at certain time periods after someone's passing away. We can offer *sadaqa* or indeed read the Holy Qur'an (see chapter 21) – and this reward can be transferred as the *ahadith* have indicated. Why would the beloved Prophet[S] instruct the Holy Qur'an to be read or offered *sadaqah* unless it benefitted the deceased?

Narrated *hazrat* Anas[R], that the Prophet[S] said, 'the Prophet's are alive in their graves and they are praying. Indeed, the prophets settle in their graves <u>after 40 nights</u> where they pray until the trumpet.' *(Mawahib Lidunya vol3 p414 & Baihaqqi)*

Thus, the reason for a 40 day *khatam* is that the soul settles in its afterlife so a boost via *du'a* is helpful, blessed and recommended. According to *hazrat* Tawoos[A] (one of the *Tabi'in* and student of Abdullah ibn Abbas[R]):

> "Indeed, the deceased are subjected to severe trials in the graves, for the first 7 days, so donate food on their behalf." *(Ahmad)*

Even the *Tabi'in* accepted and acknowledged that such assistance to those recently buried should be given. The *Tabi'in* learned from the companions[R] and the companions[R] learned from the Beloved prophet Muhammad[S]. *Khatams* are part of this process as there is great reward for completing the Holy Qur'an (*khatame-Qur'an*):

> It is reported from *Hazrat* Aa'raj that the person who completes the recitation of the Holy Qur'an from beginning then prays for its acceptance along with the fulfilment of his desires in the presence of Almighty Allah, four thousand angels say *Ameen* and they (the angels) remain engaged in the prayer (*du'a*) for the betterment and forgiveness of that person from morning to evening or from evening to morning.
> *(Tafseer Roohul Bayan, Under Verse 155 of Surah al-An'aam)*

Thus a *du'a* for the *khatam* done after the recitation of the Qur'an can benefits both the person for the deceased whom the *Esal-e-Sawab* (transfer of reward) is intended and the person or persons who help completing the reciting of the Qur'an. Or wouldn't we wish 4,000 Angels saying *Ameen* for a *du'a* made for us?

Discussion

It is already proven from Chapter 22 that: (1) We can read the Holy Qur'an for those who have passed away; (2) The deceased can receive reward as a result of those who are living (from *du'a* and *sadaqa*); (3) Good deeds can be transferred. Clearly - the living can benefit the dead.

To hold remembrance ceremonies for those who have passed away on specific days is the clear *sunnah* of Prophet Muhammad[S]. If a fresh leaf placed on the grave can benefit a person *(Bukhari 213)*, what about the recitation of the Holy Qur'an? We should make du'a for those who have passed away as we would like others to make du'a for us when we are in our graves.

25

Qs: **Why do you believe that the graves of religious people (*Mizaars*) are blessed and that they should be visited?**

Answer: Places where pious people are buried should be visited and *du'a* made as they are blessed sites as proven from Qur'an and *sunnah*.

Evidence from Holy Qur'an

"Glory be to He Who transported His Servant one night from *Masjid Haram* to *Masjid Aqsa*, <u>whose surroundings We have blessed.</u>"
(Holy Qur'an 16:1)

The underlined words emphasise the 'surroundings' that Allah^{swt} has blessed – as it is our *Qibla* (direction of prayer) and a resting place for many prophets from *Bani Israeel* (children of Israel). Therefore, all places associated with prophets or pious souls are blessed places, signs of Allah and a means of remembering him.

When prophet Zakariya^A saw *hazrate* Maryam^A getting provision he stood by her and made *du'a* for a child:

"And there, Zakariya made du'a to his Lord" *(Holy Qur'an 3:38)*

This *du'a* made at this blessed place was accepted. This is proof that making *du'a* near a saint and a place of blessing is a means for *du'a* to easily get accepted. For this reason we make *du'a* near blessed *mizaar* of *awliyaa* (saints).

"And whosoever honours the signs of Allah, that is from the piety of the hearts" *(Holy Qur'an 22:36)*

The signs of Allah^{swt} are the signs of His religion and of *taqwa* so should be visited. This is why Muslims love, venerate and seek blessings from places associated with righteous people, whether graves of the pious, mosques or historical sites. This is an expression of our piety to honour those things that are beloved to him. For example, *safa, marwah, Haramain* (*Masjid haram and nabwi shareefain*) *jannatul Baqi, Arafa, Muzdalifa, Al-Aqsaa, maqaame-Ibraheem, hajre-aswad etc* [11] - all these places have special blessings although they are inanimate objects.

Evidence from *Ahadith*

Imam Shaf'i[R] states: 'I gain the blessings from the grave of *Imam Abu Hanifa*. Whenever I got into trouble I offered two *rak'ats* and then I visited his grave, and prayed there for the solution, and *alhamdulillah* my needs were always fulfilled.' [10])

Our great scholar and guide Imam Shaf'i[R] obtained solace and guidance from the grave of Imam Abu Hanifa[R] – *subhanAllah*, what great *sufis* these wonderful Imams were.

Hazrat Abdullah[R] narrates that the holy Prophet[S] said 'I used to prohibit you from visiting graves, so visit them now for this withdraws ones attention from the world and reminds him of the hereafter.' *(Ibn Majah 1,571 & Muslim 2,131)*

It is for this reason that people visit *mizaars* - to be in the company of pious people. Because of them, their graves are blessed and our *dua's* attain blessings. It is also a fact that the dead can hear and can make *du'a* for us (see chapter 21).

According to *Imam Baihaqqi (10,299 ch346):* "*Rasoolullah*[S] regularly visited the grave of *Shuhda-e-Ahud* every year. And *hazrat* Abu Bakr Siddiq[R], *hazrat* Umar[R], *hazrat* Uthman[R] and *hazrat* Fatima[R] all used to go there and pray ". [12]

Discussion

Clearly where pious people are buried their graves are blessed as they are surrounded by Angels. Visiting blessed places is encouraged in Islam. Visiting graves of pious people is the *sunnah* of Prophet Muhammad[S] and his noble companions[R].

Pious people of the grave can pray for us (*hadith* of Musa[A] in Chapter 11). So if we wish to maximise our blessing we should visit the pious deceased, supplicate to Allah[swt] at their graves and also request their prayers. If we are totally confident of our own *taqwa* and deeds, then not visiting and making *du'a* or asking for help in this manner is an opportunity missed and our risk to take.

26

Qs: **Why do we need guides like *Shaikhs* and *peers* – why can't we go straight to Allah?**

Answer: Allah^{swt} Himself directs us towards them as they show us guidance and Allah's path.

Evidence from Holy Qur'an

"Guide us to the straight way. The path of those whom You have given blessings" *(Holy Qur'an 1:6&7)*

Allah^{swt} informs us of guidance in the noble Qur'an and also gives us the answer of who are the guided and with His blessings:

"Those upon whom Allah has bestowed his blessings are, from the prophets; the truthful; the martyrs; and the righteous. And what a noble brotherhood." *(Holy Qur'an 4:69)*

It is through these 'blessed' people that we receive guidance. The *shaikhs, peers* and *murshids* fall under the category of the 'blessed' and 'righteous'. They are those people who have been illuminated with knowledge and the ability to guide. It is indeed divine scheme that high goals in Islamic spiritualism can't be obtained individually but rather one has to have a teacher or a guide. For this Allah reminds us saying:

"Ask the people of *thikr* (remembrance), if you know not" *(Holy Qur'an 16:43)*

Allah^{swt} Himself directs us to ask others who remember Him and have knowledge. Whoever takes a profession without a teacher or master cannot succeed in any way.

"Whoever Allah sends astray will never find a guide (*walliyan murshida*)." *(Holy Qur'an 18:17)*

The word *murshid* or 'guiding teacher' appears in the Qur'an to enlighten us of the concept of a master who can show us the way towards the creator. The Qur'an states:

"Fear God and be in the company of truthful people (*Siddiqeen*)" *(Holy Qur'an 9:119)*

Allah orders us to be in the company of righteous people in order that we benefit from them by following their ways of life, their guidance and their teachings. Even Prophet Musa[A], was asked by Allah[swt] to obtain guidance from *hazrat* khidr[A], *(HQ 18:66)* even though he used to converse will Allah[swt] directly.

Evidence from *Ahadith*

Ibn Umar[R] reported that the holy Prophet[S] said, "The one who separates his hand from obedience will have no excuse on the day of judgement and he who dies without a *bay'ah* (oath of allegiance) on his neck dies the death of *jahileeyah* (ignorance)". *(Muslim 4,562)*

If there is no need to follow or take *bay'ah* (oath of allegiance) on anyone who is appointed as a leader, whether spiritual allegiance or political, the holy Prophet[S] wouldn't have stressed this concept. The noble companions[R] took allegiance on the blessed hand of the Prophet[S] for reasons that were other than political *(HQ 48:10)*.

Hazrat Abu Darda reports the holy Prophet[S] said, "Indeed, *'ulema* (scholars) are the inheritors of the prophets" *(Tirmithi 2,835)*

After the demise of the holy Prophet[S], scholars and *masha-ikh* (spiritual guides) are the beacons of light through which people are guided. They keep alive the principal of guidance and of *bay'ah*.

Discussion

It is proven from Qur'an and *sunnah* that the concept of following a *shaikh* and learning from them is essential for someone who wants to get closer to Allah[swt] and the Prophet Muhammad[S]. If one follows his desires he will surely divert from the straight path and become a 'DIY' Muslim (Do *Ijtihad* Yourself). One takes an oath of allegiance with a *shaikh* so as to fulfil the sunnah, obtain guidance and be guided to Allah[swt] and His Messenger[S].

Allah[swt] sent approximately 124,000 prophets to guide us, and approximately 313 Messengers (those with books – *Mishkaat 5,737 Ahmad 1,475*). Thus it is required for people to guide people as Allah[swt] has clearly demonstrated – and the *'Ulema* (scholars) are the inheritors of the Prophets in this regard.

27

Qs: Why do I have to follow a *madhab* – why can't I just follow Qur'an and *Sunnah*?

Answer: Following a *madhab* (way) <u>is</u> following Qur'an and *Sunnah*. You don't need to follow a *madhab* if you know more than the great Imams of the past.

Evidence from Holy Qur'an

"So ask the people of *thikr* (remembrance) if you do not know".
(Holy Qur'an 16:43)

It is clear from this verse that Allah directs us to follow those who are well versed in Islamic knowledge if we are ignorant of any religious matters. Not everyone is in a position to interpret Islamic laws.

"If they had referred it to the messenger and to <u>those with authority among them,</u> then those of them who are proper investigators (scholars) would have known" *(Holy Qur'an 4:83)*.

We are instructed to refer our matters of Islamic laws to those experts who are specialised in the fields of knowledge in order to avoid deviance. Many matters are unclear and they need knowledge, research and experts to analyse them. This is exactly what the different schools of thought stand for and following them makes following Islamic laws easier. The Holy Qur'an says:

"O you who believe, obey Allah and obey the Messenger and those in authority among you." *(Holy Qur'an 4:59)*

'Those in authority among you' is directly referring to the Jurists (Scholars) as most of us cannot be of that high calibre as our knowledge is extremely limited compared to theirs. Scholars know how to refer matters to Allah's Book and the *sunnah* and how to derive evidences, scrutinise them and give analogical deductions.

Evidence from *Ahadith*

Hudaifah[R] said that the Prophet [S] said "I do not know how long I will remain with you. So follow these two people (Who will remain) after me: *Abu Bakr and Omar*." *(Tirmithi 3,662 & Ahmed 5:382)*.

Thus, Prophet Muhammad[S] directed his companions to follow others after him who would decide as to Islamic interpretations.

The people of Madina asked *Ibn Abbas*[R] the ruling of a woman who makes (her first *tawaaf*) of the Ka'ba and thereafter experiences her menses (before she can make her final *tawaaf.) Ibn Abbas*[R] told them that she may go home without completing her final *tawaaf*. The people of Madina said, 'We will not follow your verdict and abandon the verdict of *Zayd*.' *Ibn Abbas*[R] replied, 'When you reach Madina then enquire from him...' *(Bukhari 2:625)*

The above narration clearly indicates how strictly the people of Madina held on to the verdict of *hazrat Zayd*[R]. Also note that they did not ask for any proofs as they knew his knowledgeable status. Following his ruling was following Qur'an and *sunnah*.

Hazrat Aswad bin Yazid narrates, '*Mu'adh* came to us in Yemen as a teacher and leader. We questioned him regarding a man who had passed away leaving (as his heir) a daughter and a sister. He gave half the estate for the daughter and half for the sister.' *(Bukhari 2,477)*

The people of Yemen would ask *Hazrat Muadh*[R] but never used to ask for proofs as they knew him as an authority. As a matter of fact the companions would even exhort the people to do *taqlid shakhsi* (blind following). When people came to ask Abu Musa[R] a question he said to them, 'Do not ask me as long as this erudite scholar (*'Abdullah ibn Mas'ud*) is present amongst you.' *(Bukhari 2,477)*

Discussion

The Prophet[S] sent many Companions to different communities and these people restricted themselves only to the views of that companion. They would follow his verdicts without questioning as he was a man of knowledge and practice. One cannot extract the principals of Islamic laws from Qur'an and sunnah unless one is well versed in the relevant sciences. That is why people follow a *madhab*.

If a person thinks they know everything and can establish their own individual school of thought then they are arrogant and misguided. These 'DIY' Muslims (Do *Ijtihad* Yourself) are following slogans not proper guidance and will usually be misguided.

28

Qs: Following a *waseela* (intermediary) is *shirk*, we should go straight to Allah

Answer: Using an intermediary is part of Islam and it is proven from Qur'an and *sunnah*.

Evidence from Holy Qur'an

"O you who believe fear Allah <u>and seek a *waseelah*</u> (intermediary) to approach Him and struggle in his way..." *(Holy Qur'an 5:35)*

Allah clearly requires us to find a *waseela*, referring to pious people acting as intermediaries. The verse then continues to discuss actions and deeds which are also.

"When they had been unjust to themselves, <u>they should go to you</u> (O Prophet^S) and asked Allah's forgiveness and the Messenger would ask forgiveness for them, indeed they would have found the doors of Allah's mercy open. *(Holy Qur'an 4:64)*

Verily in this verse Allah directs people to the holy prophet^S if they have sinned. This is an instruction from Allah^swt to seek intercession through the holy prophet^S. Allah^swt is certainly near but He Himself is directing us to the holy prophet^S. This verse shows the proof of *tawassul* in the light of Holy Qur'an – and this is undeniable.

"And when there come to them a book from Allah confirming what is with them and the *Injeel* (Bible), although for a period of time they invoked (through Muhammad^S) in order to gain victory over disbelievers" *(Holy Qur'an 2:89)*

Imam Qurtubi (in relation to the above verse) relates the tradition through Ibn 'Abbas: The Jews of Khaybar were often at war with the *Ghatafan* (tribe). When they confronted each other (in battle) the Jews were defeated. They attacked again, offering this prayer, "(O Lord,) we beg you <u>through the intercession of the unlettered Prophet</u> about whom You have promised that you will send him at the end of time. Please help us against them." Ibn 'Abbas adds: whenever they faced the enemy they offered this prayer and defeated the *Ghatafan* (tribe). But when the Prophet^S was sent, they denied (him). So Allah the Exalted revealed the verse (as above), that is, through your mediation, O Muhammad^S. *(Tafseer Qurtubi, al-Jami li Ahkam al-Qur'an)*

56

Evidence from *Ahadith*

Narrated from 'Uthman bin Hunaif that a blind man came to the Prophet[S] and said: 'Pray to Allah to heal me.' He said: 'If you wish to store your reward for the Hereafter, that is better, or if you wish, I will make *du'a* (supplicate) for you.' He said: 'Supplicate.' So he told him to perform ablution and do it well, to pray two *rak'ah*, and to say this *du'a*: 'O Allah, I ask of You and I turn my face towards You by virtue of the intercession of Muhammad the Prophet of mercy. O Muhammad[S], (*yaa* Muhammad[S]) I have turned to my Lord by your intercession about this need of mine so that it may be met. O Allah, accept his intercession concerning me'. *(Ibn Majah 1,385)*

The Prophet Muhammad[S] taught this *du'a* – that help should be obtained by calling upon His blessed name actually within the *du'a*. *Hazrat* Adam[A] also sought forgiveness through his blessed *waseela*:

Narrated 'Umar[R], the Prophet[S] said, 'When Adam[A] committed his mistake he said: 'O my Lord, I am asking you to forgive me for the sake of Muhammad...' [22]

Hazrat 'Umar[R] used to ask for rain using the name of Prophet Muhammad[S] and his blessed uncle:

Whenever drought threatened them Umar bin Al-Khattab[R] used to ask Abbas bin Abdul Muttalib[R] to invoke Allah for rain. He used to say, 'O Allah! We have been (continuously) invoking you for rain through the Prophet[S] and you would bless us with rain, and now we ask you through the uncle of your prophet[S]. 'O Allah! Bless us with rain', he said, and so it would rain.' *(Bukhari 1,010)*

Discussion

Seeking a *waseela* (intermediary) is instructed by Allah[swt] and Prophet Muhammad[S], so it cannot be deemed *shirk*. This would make every Muslim a *mushrik*, because all our affairs require intermediaries. The Prophet[S] received revelation through the *waseela* of Jibraeel[A] – was this *shirk?*' The Prophet[S] would also be requested to make du'a for various companions and he did so – was this *shirk?*. In our *du'a* after *athaan*, we also ask that our beloved Prophet Muhammad[S] is our *waseela* *(Bukhari 614)*. Thus, through him, Allah[swt] answers our *du'a*.

57

29

Qs: Only Prophets can perform miracles, *'Awliyaa'* cannot. Why do you say that they can?

Answer: The Holy Qur'an and the narrations of the Prophet[S] prove that *Awliyaa* (friends of Allah) can perform miracles.

Evidence from Holy Qur'an

"(O Maryam) Shake the trunk of the palm tree towards you, and it will let fall fresh ripe dates upon you." *(Holy Qur'an 19:25)*

Here we have a great and pious woman and non-prophet *hazrat* Maryam[R] a friend of Allah (*Waliyyatullah*) perform a miracle. She was instructed to shake a part of a palm tree that was withered, dry and dead. Allah[swt] in this verse stated that through her blessed touch, the ripe and fresh dates were presented. Such is the standing of the *Awliyaa Ikram* (noble friends of Allah) be they male or female. When Prophet Sulaiman[A] requested someone to perform a miracle and bring the throne of Bilqees, then:

"One with whom was knowledge of the scripture said, "I will bring it to you before the twinkling of the eye" then (prophet Sulaiman) saw it placed before him." *(Holy Qur'an 27:40)*.

It is evident from the above verse the power and miracles of the *awliya* of Allah. The pious man (a non-prophet) brought the throne of Bilqees in the blink of an eye. *Hazrat* Suleiman went on to say this is from the blessings of Allah.

Evidence from *Ahadith*

"When Sa'd (ibn Abi Waqqas) and the Muslim army arrived at the Tigris River during the battle of Qadisiyyah, Salman stopped and said: "A river from the rivers of Allah. Will it not carry the soldiers of Allah?" So, he took Sa'd by the hand and stepped onto the water, leading all 30,000 soldiers across the Tigris River on foot. The Persians saw this and escaped, saying: "The demons have arrived! The demons have arrived!". *(Tarikh Tabari Vol.3, No.323)*

If a man or men are close enough to Allah^{swt} then this hadith shows how exactly they can be bestowed with the most amazing and astounding miracles imaginable. The *sahaaba-ikram*^{R} were clearly not Prophets, and yet this amongst countless other *ahadith* demonstrate how they were blessed recipients of miraculous acts.

Sayyidina 'Umar sent his army to Persia. The army occupied by the enemy near *Nahhwaand Sayyidina* 'Umar advised his commander standing on the *mimbar* (pulpit) in Madina while he was addressing a public gathering. He said, 'O Sariyah! Towards the mountain!'. *Nihawaand* was miles away from Madinah but he heard the voice. *(Baihaqqi, Mishkaat 5,954, Hujjahtullaahi 'Alal-'Aalamiin 612)*

The amazing voice of *hazrat* 'Umar^R when speaking from Madinah *Munawwara* was heard by *hazrat* Sariyah hundreds of miles away *mashaAllah*.

On the authority of *hazrat* Anas^R, 'Usaid bin Hudair^R and 'Abbad nin Bishr^R were talking with *rasoolullah*^{S} until it became dark. They left for their homes and each had a stick in their hand. The stick of one illuminated the way and when they separated the other stick illuminated and each walked by the light of his stick. *(Mishkaat 5,944, Bukhari 8:454)*

Clearly, two companions^R were blessed so much that they had their own sustainable torches made from wood! *Subhanallah*.

There is also a *hadith* in which the quantity of food in the house of Abu Bakr^R increased so he could feed his guests *mashaAllah* with the remainder being many times more than the original amount. Food for 3 people, became food for 12 groups of people. *(Mishkaat 5,946, Bukhari 576, Muslim 5,106)*

Discussion

Clearly from the above we can see that the statement that only Prophets can perform miracles is wrong. All true *Awliya* who exist in the creation till the Day of Judgement have the ability to perform miracles, but not all perform them. The miracles performed by the Prophets are called "*mu'jiza*" (miracles) and those performed by Awliyaa are called "*Karamat*" (noble events).

59

30

Qs: Why do you call you yourselves '*Ahle sunnah wal jamaa'ah'* (people of *sunnah* and the majority) when we should call ourselves 'Muslims'?

Answer: It is sunnah to call the true followers and lovers of the holy Prophet[S] as *ahle-sunah wal jamaa'ah*.

Evidence from Holy Qur'an

"O you who believe fear Allah as he should be feared and die not except in a state of Islam. And hold fast to the rope of Allah and do not be separated." *(Holy Qur'an 3:103)*

The unity of Muslims is the utmost important thing. The rightly guided group of Muslims is that which is united under the banner of the holy Qur'an, the traditions of the holy Prophet[S] and his companions[R].

"On the Day of Judgement, some people's faces will be bright, and others will be dark" *(Holy Qur'an 3:106)*

It is reported that Abdullah ibn Abbas[R] said regarding the verse "Those whose faces will be bright will be *Ahl us-Sunnah wal Jama'ah*, and those whose faces will be dark will be *Ahl Al Bid'ah wal Firqah.*" *(Tafseer Tabari and Ibn Kathir under the said Ayah).* (*ahlul bid'ah wal firqah* means 'the people of (bad) innovation and sects/groups)

Clearly, the phrase, *ahle sunnah wal jama'ah*, is part of the vocabulary of Abdullah ibn Abbas[R], who is the cousin of Prophet Muhammad[S]. Allah[swt] granted him understanding of *deen* and sciences (*tafseer*) of Holy Qur'an *(Muslim 6,523).* If it was his vocabulary, then it would also be the vocabulary of the *Sahaabah ikraam* (noble companions).

Evidence from *Ahadith*

In the following hadith, the holy Prophet[S] is reported to have instructed us to follow the jamaa'ah.

Hazrat Awfu bin Malik narrates that the holy prophet said, the Jews divided into 71 sects, 1 is in *jannah* and 70 are in hellfire, the Christians were divided in to 72 sects 1 is in *jannah* and 71 in hellfire. By the one whose hand my soul is in my ummah will be divided into 73 sects.72 are in hellfire. The *sahabah* asked who are the saved sects. He said "*al jamaa'ah*" (*Ibn Majah 3,982*)

Al-jamaa'ah refers to the majority. Since there are various groups of Muslims *al-jamaa'ah* is that group of people who follow the Prophet[S] and his companions[R] and those that came after them.

The holy Prophet[S] said there is going to be calamity after calamity, whoever you see leaving the *jamaa'ah* or wants to divide you when you are united under the *jamaa'ah*, kill him whoever he is. Allah's hand is over the *jamaa'ah*. *Shaitan* is far from the *jamaa'ah*. (*Muslim 1,847 Bukhari 6,557*)

The Beloved Prophet[S] said, "Allah will never allow my Ummah to unite upon misguidance and incorrect beliefs. Allah's mercy, blessings and protection are with the largest group of Muslims. And he who deviates from this largest group of Muslims will be thrown into Hell." (*Tirmithi 2,256, 2,255 & 2,167*)

Thus, the majority are correct and it is the majority who follow the *aqaaid* (beliefs) explained in this booklet and are *ahle sunnah wal jamaa'ah*.

Discussion

Division among the ummah was prophesised and inevitable. So to stay upon the true path we must separate ourselves from the various misguided sects. This is done under the name of *Ahle sunnah wal Jamaa'ah*, which is the biggest congregation of the Muslims. From this we can gather that Allah has willed for the truth to be kept within the largest group of Muslims.

The majority of Muslims are in the group *Ahle-sunhan wal jama'ah* and they are those who follow the *aqeeda* described in this booklet and not those who simply say they are a member. Their actions and beliefs decide their membership not their words. Quite simply, those who demonstrate tremendous love, honour and respect of Prophet Muhammad[S] are the *Ahle-sunhan wal jama'ah*.

61

31

Qs: **Prove that there are *Qutb Ghawth*, *Abdaal* and that they control the world.**

Answer: These are high ranks of the *awliyaa* of Allah[swt] (friends of Allah) who have been mentioned in the prophetic traditions.

Evidence from Holy Qur'an

"Behold , verily the *Awliyaa* of Allah have no fear nor grief."
(Holy Qur'an 10:62)

The co existence of the *awliyaa*-Allah is mentioned in the Holy Qur'an and these are those people who have attained high ranks and great proximity to Allah[swt] in worship and obedience.

"...Allah will elevate in degree those of you who believe and those who have been given knowledge." *(Holy Qur'an 58:11)*

Verily the Almighty elevates believers in accordance to their knowledge and belief to different ranks as clearly mentioned in the holy book. Clearly, these levels have names. We know of a few 'levels' such as Prophets, Messengers, Companions, and *awliyaa*.

"Above every knowledgeable one there is *one* more knowledgeable" *(Holy Qur'an 12:76)*

It is clear from the above verse that knowledge will never be equal, there is always that person who is more knowledgeable whether in *Shari'ah* or spiritual knowledge and through this we see different ranks of the *Aqtaab*, *Ghawth* and *Abdaal* – some of the names of levels of the *awliyaa ikraam*.

Evidence from *Ahadith*

The prophet Muhammad[S], mentioned one of these people as having powers of governing the earth, these number 7 and are known as the 'Qutb' or *Aqtaab*:

Narrated Abu Hurairah[R], 'One day I joined the Messenger[S] of Allah.
He told me that in a few moments a man is going to come to me through that door, who is <u>one of the seven</u> through whom God protects

the inhabitants of the earth. An Ethiopian (*habashi*) then entered the door. He was bald and his nose was short and he carried a jar of water on his head. The Messenger[S] of God said, 'O Abu Hurairah[R], it's him.' He told him three times, 'welcome Yasar!' This man used to sprinkle the mosque and sweep it. He was the young servant of Mughira bin shu'ba. [13]

Hazrat Ali[R] has informed us about the *abdaal* who are another category of *awliyaa ikram*:

Imam Ahmad[R] narrates, 'The people of Syria were mentioned in front of `Ali ibn Abi Talib[R] while he was in Iraq, and they said, 'Curse them, O Commander of the Believers.' He replied, 'No, I heard the Messenger[S] of Allah say, 'The Substitutes (*al-abdaal*) are in Syria and they are forty men, every time one of them dies, Allah substitutes another in his place. By means of them Allah brings down the rain, gives (Muslims) victory over their enemies, and averts punishment from the people of Syria. *(Ahmad 898)*

Imam Ahmad bin Hambal[R] and Imam Tabarani[R] have also told us one of the names of the levels of *awliyaa-ikraam* – the *abdaal* or 'substitutes'.

Imam Ahmad bin Hambal[R] relates from Ubada bin samit, 'The *abdaal* in this community are thirty, their hearts are in affinity with that of *hazrat* Ibrahim, the intimate friend of Allah the All Merciful, each time one of them dies. *(Musnad Ahmad 5:322)*

'Ubada bin al samit[R] narrates, 'The *abdaal* of this ummah are thirty, it is through them the earth is maintained, the rains come to you and you receive God assistance.' *(Tabarani & Suyuti [14])*

Discussion

The categories of these special, spiritual men - their responsibilities, names and even numbers are evident from the above narrations. The term *Ghouth* (healer) is also a title for one such great personality. The fact that Allah has elevated their status amongst men, is proof of their position. It is through them that we receive rain and the assistance of Allah[swt], protection, and above all gain victory over our enemies. This is how Allah[swt] wishes to mange His system so we should not deny it.

32

Qs: **Prove from Qur'an and Hadith that *Ta'weeth* (protection) are allowed, especially when Allah specifically forbids wearing amulets?**

Answer: *Ta'weeth* is a written *du'a* from Holy Qur'an or hadith for spiritual treatment. It is clearly permissible from the time of Prophet Muhammad[S].

Evidence from Holy Qur'an

"And we have revealed from Qur'an that which is a healing and mercy for those who believe."*(Holy Qur'an 17:82)*

Allah described that from the holy Qur'an there are special verses as *shifaa* (healing or cure). This means that they have so much power they can cure people from physical and spiritual illnesses.

Evidence from *Ahadith*

Amr ibn Shu'aib narrates from his father who narrates from his grandfather Abdullah ibn Amr[R] that *Rasulullah*[S] said, "When anyone of you gets frightened in his sleep, let him recite this du'a,' (then he mentioned the *du'a*) so Abdullah Ibn 'Amar[R] would teach this du'a to those of his children who could read. As for those who could not, he would write it and <u>hang it around their necks</u>". *(Musannaf Ibn Abi Shaibah vol5 p439, Tirmithi 3,539) [15]*

Thus, in the time of the holy Prophet[S] his companions[R] would write and place these *du'a* around the necks of their children for their protection. The Holy Prophet[S] himself would recite the Holy Qur'an and blow upon the sick and by the grace of Allah they would get treated *(Bukhari 631& 634).*

Imam Hajjaj[R] says, 'Those who saw *Sayyiduna Sa'eed ibn Jubair* [R] writing *ta'weeth* for those who came to him related to me (regarding this matter), Imam Hajjaj[R] further says, 'I asked Ataa regarding it.' He replied, 'We have not heard anyone disliking it but from you, the people of Iraq". *(Ibn Abi Shaiba vol5 p434)*

Thus, a great *Tab'ee* (successors of the *sahabah*) like 'Ataa, who was the Mufti of Makkah at a time when the *sahabah* were still present denied hearing anyone disliking the usage of ta'weeth. If he was aware that it is *shirk* and *bid'ah* – he would have said something. Auf Ibn Malik[R] says:

> "We would use amulets (*Ruqyah*) in the days of ignorance, so we asked *Rasoolullah*[S] regarding it", he said "bring to me your amulets, thereafter he said: 'There is nothing wrong with amulets if they do not contain *shirk* (in them)". *(Muslim 5,457)*

Thus those amulets forbidden are only those associated with false gods, NOT those with Qur'anic verses or *du'a* as these relate to Allah and His Messenger[S]. This has been clearly approved by Prophet Muhammad[S]. This has been discussed at length by Imam Qurtubi[R] [15].

> Narrated Alaqah ibn Sahar at-Tamimi[R]: We left the Apostle of Allah for a clan of the Arabs. They asked, '...Have you any medicine or a charm, for we have a lunatic in chains?' We said: 'Yes,' so they brought the lunatic in chains. I recited *Surah al-Faatiha* over him for three days, morning and evening. Whenever I finished it I would collect my saliva and spit it out, and he seemed as if he were set free from a bond. They gave me some payment, but I said, 'Not until I ask the Apostle of Allah'. He (the Prophet[S]) said: 'Accept it, for by my life, some accept it for a worthless charm, but you have done so for a genuine one.' *(Abu Daood 3,413 & 3,892)*

Thus, again, clearly the beloved prophet Muhammad[S] allowed spiritual healing and also allowed payment for it. There is again a clear distinction between a *halal ta'weeth* and a *haram* one.

Discussion

It was clearly the practice of *sahabah*[R] and *tabi'een*[R] to write *du'a* on a piece of paper and place it around the neck of a person for protection. Of course, the du'a is from the Holy Qur'an and *ahadith* have the power to heal the sick.

The *ta'weeth* that are forbidden are those from the time of Ignorance, which are satanic and contain an element of *shirk* (mantar, voodoo and magic, etc.). The *ta'weeth*, which are permitted are those written with du'a and are in conformity with Qur'an and *ahadith*.

33

Qs: Any *bid'a* (innovation) is bad. There is no such thing as a good *bid'ah*?

Answer: Innovations is of two types: good and bad. Bad is that which opposes Qur'an and *sunnah*. Good is that which is in accordance with Qur'an and *sunnah*.

Evidence from Holy Qur'an

"And we ordained in the hearts of those who followed him Compassion and Mercy. But the Monasticism which <u>they innovated for themselves</u> which we did not prescribe for them, but they sought it only to please Allah..." *(Holy Qur'an 57:27)*

Innovating to please Allah^{swt} is permissible and it should be in accordance with Qur'an and *Sunnah*. Allah^{swt} rewarded those who believed as they did right.

Evidence from *Ahadith*

Jareer ibn 'Abdullaah al-Bajali said, 'The Messenger^S of Allah said: <u>'Whoever introduces a new thing in Islam will receive the reward for it</u> and the reward for those who act upon it, without detracting from their reward in any way. Whoever starts a bad thing will bear the sin of it and the sin for those who follow him...' *(Tirmithi 2,675)*

Thus, it is clearly permissible to introduce some new action and for others to follow that new action. This is of course with the proviso that it is in accordance with Qur'an and Sunnah. If Allah^{swt} likes this action, he will make it flourish. This does not mean Islam is incomplete as this hadith makes it a *sunnah* – thus with this *sunnah* it is complete.

'Abdur Rahman bin 'Abdul Qari said, "I went out in the company of 'Umar bin Al-Khattab one night in Ramadan to the mosque and found the people praying in different and separate groups....So, 'Umar said, 'In my opinion I would collect these (people) under one Reciter' (i.e. make them pray in congregation). So, he made them congregate behind Ubai bin Ka'b. Then on another night I went again in his company and the people were praying behind their reciter. On that, 'Umar remarked, 'What an excellent *Bid'a* (innovation) this is (*ni'mal bid'atu haathi hee*)." *(Bukhari 32:227)*

Hazrat 'Umar[R] (who is known as *Farooq* – who distinguishes between right and wrong [16]) said that his introduction of this practise of reading *Tarawih* prayer in congregation and said that it is a good bid'ah (*ni'mal bid'ah*). Thus he introduced something which he called a 'good *bid'ah*' which is clearly beneficial for the Muslims rather than allow them to pray in small groups. We still follow this '*bid'ah*' today.

During the caliphate of Abu Bakr , 'Umar came to Abu Bakr and said: 'In the Battle of Yamama many *Huffaath* of Qur'an have been Martyred. I fear that if this continues the Qur'an would disappear. You should command for the Qur'an to be collected'. He replied: 'How can I do a thing, which was not a practice of *Rasoolallah.*' Umar replied: 'By Allah this is a good thing,' and he mentioned this many times to the *Khalifa*. Later Abu Bakr said: 'Allah has opened my heart to the fact that although this was not an action of *Rasoolallah,* it is a good thing'. Abu Bakr then told Zaid to start collecting the Qur'an who questioned the *Khalifa* by asking: 'Why are you doing something which was not an action of the holy prophet?' *Hazrat* Abu Bakr replied: 'By Allah this is a very good thing.' Zaid later said: 'Allah opened my heart to the fact that this was a good thing so I started collecting the Qur'an until it was collected.' *(Bukhari 60:201).*

Thus, the Qur'an we read as a book was collated by the companions as it was a good thing to do. If they had not introduced this practice, then? Definitely a good *bid'ah*.

Discussion

Hazrat 'Umar ordered the people to offer congregational prayers of *Taraweeh*, and called this a blessed *bid'ah*. *Hazrat* 'Umar saw the writing of Holy Qur'an as a benefit to the ummah for it wasn't there in the time of the holy prophet[S] and *hazrat* Abu Bakr[R] and *hazrat* Zaid[R] felt it was a good thing to do. Even after that another good innovation was brought by placing punctuation marks. Introducing new, good things in Islam has been sanctioned by Prophet Muhammad[S] himself and practiced by his companions[R].

All these practices, however, must follow Qur'an and *sunnah* and the *'Ulema* should accept these practices. Thus they are permissible as in reality, evidence can be found for them.

34

Qs: Prove that *du'a* can be said in congregation after prayer

Answer: To make *du'a* in congregation is the *sunnah*.

Evidence from Holy Qur'an

"And seek forgiveness from all-together, O believers, that you may be successful" *(Holy Qur'an 24:31)*

Allah commands *du'a* to be made together in this verse. If supplicating in congregation was forbidden then the Almighty Allah would have addressed believers to do this action individually.

"Verily the invocation of both of you is accepted (O Musa and Harun)!" *(Holy Qur'an 10: 89)*

Supplicating collectively is permissible according to the Holy Qur'an. The reports from the noble companions[R] and *Salaf* concur that this type of supplication was that Musa[A] supplicated while Harun[A] said *Ameen*, as narrated by the Imams of *Tafseer* from Ibn Abbas[A], Abu Hurairah[A], Abu Salih, and others [17].

Evidence from *Ahadith*

Abu Umama al-Bahili[R] narrates: The Messenger[S] of Allah was asked as to which supplication (*du'a*) was most quickly accepted? He replied: 'In the middle of the night and after the obligatory (*fard*) prayers'. *(Tirmithi, 5:188 with a sound (hasan) chain of transmission).*

It is evident from this *hadith* that supplication after every *fard* prayer is very powerful as authentically proven from the teachings of the holy Prophet[S]. This is thus a *sunnah* and a highly recommended act and should be followed.

Habib ibn Maslama al-Fihri[A] narrates that I heard the Messenger[S] of Allah say: 'No group of believers assemble, one of them supplicating while others saying *ameen*, except that Allah answers their prayers'. *(Tabrani in al-Mujum al-Kabir, 4:26 & al-Mustadrak, 3:347)*

It is clear from the above *hadith* that in assemblies where believers gather there is nothing more virtuous than the *du'a* in congregation where the imam makes *du'a* and others say *ameen* in response.

Anas ibn Malik[R] narrates that a villager came to the Messenger[S] of Allah on Friday and said: 'O Messenger of Allah, the livestock are dying, the dependents are dying, and the people are dying.' The Messenger[S] of Allah raised his hands in supplication and the people raised their hands in supplication with him. *(Bukhari 13:54)*

Abu Shaddad[R] narrates while Ubada ibn al-Samit[R] was present and confirmed him. We were in the house of the Messenger[S] of Allah when he said: 'Is there any stranger among you?' He meant one from the People of the Book. We said, 'No, O Messenger of Allah'. He ordered for the door to be shut and said: 'Raise your hands and say *Laa ilaaha illAllah*'. We raised our hands for a while. Then he said: 'O Allah! Truly You have sent me with this phrase and promised me Paradise for it. Truly, You do not break the trust'. Then he said: 'Be glad, for Allah has forgiven you'. *(Ahmad 4:124)*

It clearly evident that the Prophet[S] would raise his hands and the companions[R] would do the same with him. So it's clear that collective *du'a* is approved from the *sunnah*.

Ibn 'Abbas reported, 'Ask from Allah with the palms of your hands (upward) and do not ask Him with the backs and when you have finished wipe your faces with them.' *(Abu Daood 1,480, 1,481-1,487 & Tirmithi 3,386)*

So collective *du'a* after prayer, raising ones hands for *du'a*, *du'a* after prayer and wiping ones faces is all *sunnah*.

Discussion

It is clear that making *du'a* by raising ones hands and in congregation is permissible and is the *sunnah* of Prophet Muhammad[S]. As the best *du'a* is made after compulsory prayers, it would be negligent of us not to maximise our reward. Thus if the Imam makes a *du'a* then we should join him. Those who still object after these evidences will miss a clear *sunnah* and are denying themselves benefit from this noble act.

Note also that when the Imam recites *surah faatiha* in congregation, he is making a *du'a* and we are say *ameen*. *Du'a-qunoot* is also said in *fajr* prayers by the followers of *Imam* Shaf'i by raising their hands collectively and saying *ameen* – or is this wrong as well?

35

Qs: What is the evidence of doing congregational *thikr* after prayers and at functions?

Answer: Congregational *thikr* is approved from Holy Qur'an and *sunnah* whether after prayers or at functions.

Evidence from Holy Qur'an

"Then when you have completed the acts of Hajj, remember Allah as you used to remember your fathers". *(Holy Qur'an 2:200)*

Commentators of the Holy Qur'an say that in the era of ignorance, it was the practice of the *Kuffaar* that after they completed their Hajj rituals, they would stand in front of the *Ka'bah* and praise their forefathers aloud. In this *ayah*, Allah[swt] says that they should mention Allah instead. Therefore, it is understandable that this *thikr*, which is performed has to be loud so that people will be able to listen to it.

"Remember me, I shall remember you." *(Holy Qur'an 2:152)*

Allah did not mention any condition of remembrance whether loud or soft, individually or in a group. Thus we have no right to put conditions on them. (They should be understood as general statements and should not be made conditional.)

"And the remembrance of Allah is the greatest..." *(HQ 29:45)*

Evidence from *Ahadith*

Narrated Abu Ma'bad (the freed slave of Ibn 'Abbas) Ibn 'Abbas told me, 'In the lifetime of the Prophet it was the customary to celebrate Allah's praises aloud after the compulsory congregational prayers.' Ibn 'Abbas further said, 'When I heard the *thikr*, I would learn that the compulsory congregational prayer had ended.' *(Bukhari 12:802 and similar in Muslim 1,211 & Mishkaat)*

Clearly, reciting *thikr* aloud and in congregation after *salah* is the *sunnah*. This *thikr* was loud, together and approved.

Abu Hurairah[R] reported: The Messenger[S] of Allah said, 'Allah the Exalted says: 'I am where my slave expects me to be, and I am with him when he remembers Me. If he remembers Me inwardly, I will remember him inwardly, and if he remembers Me in an assembly, I will remember him in a better assembly (i.e., in the assembly of angels)." *(Bukhari 12:802, Muslim 1,211)*

MashaAllah, such is the blessing of the gathering of *thikr* that Allah[swt] remembers those who are remembering Him! How can then anyone object to such a noble act?

Abu Hurairah[R] and Hazrat Abu Sa'eed[R] testify (upon oath) that *Rasulullah*[S] said: 'Any group of people who engage in the *thikr* of Allah, the angels envelop them and mercy cascades upon them, tranquillity descends upon them and Allah remembers them in the presence of those who are by Him. *(Muslim 6,471 & 6,498, Tirmithi 3,389 [18])*

So, if we wish the Angels to surround us and the mercy of Allah to fall upon us then we know what to do.

Zaid bin Aslam reports from a *Sahabi* that, 'One night I walked with *Rasulullah*[S] when he passed by a person in the *masjid* who was engaged in loud *thikr*. I said, 'O Messenger[S] of Allah, perhaps he is showing-off.' He replied, 'No but in fact he is an *Awwaah*.'
(Baihaqqi – Shu'bal Iman)

(*Awwaah* is that person who experiences pangs of pain in the heart or experience ecstasy due to overwhelming and ardent love for Allah [19]. Doing *thikr* loudly has clearly been approved by the Prophet Muhammad[S]. If it was wrong, he would have stopped him rather than explain and allow him to continue and also praise him.

Discussion

There has been no argument over the issue of congregational zikr among Muslim scholars until ignorant Muslims speak to try and stop the remembrance of Allah. Countless traditions points out that it was a practice of our pious predecessors.

It is also evident from the narration of *hazrat* Abdullah Ibn Abbas[R] that they used to realise that *salah* is finished when they would hear loud, congregational *thikr* inside the Masjid.

36 Qs: What is the evidence for celebrating 'Urs?

Answer: 'Urs is a commemoration of the passing away of the noble Saints[R] and Prophets[A]. The word 'Urs has been taken from Hadith to signify total peace of the pious saints in *barzakh*.

Evidence from Holy Qur'an

"O Allah! Our Lord, send down upon us a tray from the Heaven so that it should be a festival for us, for the first one of us and the last one of us." *(Holy Qur'an 5:114)*

This verse indicates that we should rejoice on the day of receiving a bounty, and honouring and respecting that it is counted among the teachings the Prophets, and a source of Allah's Pleasure. *(Tafseer Kabeer & Tafseer Roohul Bayan.)* To rejoice on the day of the demise of the noble Saints and the pious men is meritorious because it is the day that they obtain "union" with Allah the almighty.

"We are your helpers in this world and in the hereafter." *(HQ 41:31)*

The angels are always in the company of pious people in this world in *barzakh* and the hereafter. They reside in blessed places and are places of attaining spirituality and intercession. The blessings the pious attain are not restricted to this world. The *ayah* continues to tell us that they also receive blessings in the hereafter and to us they are sources of attaining blessings also.

"And mention in the book the story of Maryam..." *(Holy Qur'an 19:16)*

Allah[swt] mentions *hazrate* Maryam[A] in the Holy Qur'an even though she wasn't a prophet but we are instructed to remember her and remember her great story. Thus to narrate and remember such stories in a gathering fulfils this commandment.

"O you who believe! Take not as friends the people who incurred the wrath of Allah. Surely, they have despaired of the Hereafter, just as the disbelievers have despaired of the people of the graves." *(Holy Qur'an 60:13)*

Therefore, only those who disbelieve have issues with those who are deceased and their graves. Thus, we should not be like them but should honour such pious people as was the *sunnah* of Prophet Muhammad[S].

Evidence from *Ahadith*

The Prophet Muhammad used to go to the graves of the martyrs of 'Uhd once a year and also recite the verse of the Holy Qur'an on excellence of patience. The Prophet Muhammad used to pray for them. When the beloved Prophet Muhammad passed away himself, the Khalifs, Abu-Bakr, Umar, Usman used to do the same thing. (*Tafsir Tabari, Tafsir Ibn-Kathir, Tafsir Qurtabi, (by Imam Tabari) on HQ 13:20 & Shaami in Baabu Ziyaaratil-Quboor)..* [12]

It has become evident from this that the noble Companions celebrated the *'Urs* of the Holy Prophet[S]. (Also see Chapter 13)

The Angels (*Munkar*[A] & *Nakeer*[A]) when questioning pious souls, say, *'nam ka-nawma-til 'uroos'* or 'Sleep just like the newly married sleep.' *(Tirmithi 1,073, Mishkaat 130).* Thus, a celebration of 'Urs is simply a celebration of the beautiful and peaceful time of a pious saint in *barzakh*.

Discussion

On the day of the passing away of a Saint or on a specific date, his admirers, disciples, followers and relatives assemble together at the grave of the Saint to obtain spiritual benefit and celebrate the anniversary with rejoice.

It is for this reason that on the date or the day the Muslim Saint passes away *'Urs* of a *Wali* is set aside for their commemoration or celebration. People go to the graves of the Friends of Allah (*awliyaa*) to seek blessings and out of love for them, stand before the graves of the Saints and pray to Allah through the intercession.

It is also the case that the *awliyaa ikram* can make *du'a* for the person requesting assistance as proven by the *hadith* of Musa[A] when he was seen standing and praying in his grave *(Muslim 5,858 and Chapter 11).*

37

Qs: Why do you celebrate things like *Giyarvee* when there is no evidence for this?

Answer: *Giyarwee Shareef* is specifically an *Esaale-Sawaab* for *Sayyidina Shaikh* Abdul Qadir Jilani.

Evidence from Holy Qur'an

"And follow the way of those who have turn to me" *(HQ 31:15)*

Allah[swt] informs us to follow the way of those who have turned to him. These are his servants who contributed immensely to the progress and propagation of religion. They are great luminaries and examples to follow. *Shaykh 'Abd al-Qaadir*[R] is one of the *imaams* of Islam and a great saint. He attained a position of leadership over the Muslims in his time, in knowledge, good deeds, issuing *fatawaa* and other aspects of religion. He was one of the greatest *mashaa-ikh* of all time, enjoining adherence to the *Shari'ah*, enjoining what is good, forbidding what is evil, and giving that precedence over all else. He was an ascetic *(zaahid)* and a preacher, in whose gatherings many people repented. Allah[swt] caused him to be well-liked by people and his virtues became widely-known – may Allah bestow abundant mercy upon him.

"Those upon whom Allah has bestowed his blessing, from the prophets; the truthful, the martyrs; and the righteous. And what a noble brotherhood!" *(Holy Qur'an 4:69)*

Indeed Allah[swt] has praised the righteous of this *ummah* and ordered us to follow their footsteps. Remembering them in our *du'as* and gatherings is advisable as we speak of their good deeds. This action of gathering to remember this great saint is the essence of the *Giyarwee Shareef* where in fact all Muslims are remembered for *Esaale-Sawaab*. It is also celebrated on the 11th of every Islamic Month (*Giyarwee* means eleven in Urdu) in many mosques or by individuals at home. This auspicious function takes place both nationally and internationally endowing great spiritual benefits and *barakah*. The great Shaikh himself set aside this time each month

(11th) to promote Islam to the masses – a practice which his admirers honour and follow to this day.

Evidence from *Ahadith*

Abud-Dardaa^R reported: 'I heard the Messenger of Allah say: And verily, the virtue of the scholar over the worshipper is like the virtue of the moon on the night of Al-Badr over all of the stars. Indeed, the scholars are the inheritors of the prophets, for the prophets do not leave behind a dinar or a dirham for inheritance, but rather, they leave behind knowledge. So whoever takes hold of it, has acquired a large share (i.e. of inheritance)'. *(Mishkaat 212, Tirmithi 2,691, Ahmad, Abu Daood, Ibn Majah & Daarimi 342)*

The scholars are guides to mankind. They possess knowledge of the Laws of Allah^{swt}, have understanding of His religion and who act by their knowledge and *taqwa*. The scholars are those who possess a deep understanding of Islam, around whom revolve the giving of religious verdicts (*fatawaa*); who extract rulings; and who lay down precise principles which determine the lawful from the prohibited.

The scholars are the inheritors of the Prophets. They inherited from them knowledge which they carry in their hearts demonstrate in their actions. *Shaikh* Abdul Qadir Jilani^R was a great scholar and a great Muslim saint. It is for this reason that many love him and commemorate *gyarwee shareef* to attain spiritual benefits.

Discussion

A saintly individual and *sayyid* from both his parents, he was a spiritual and intellectual giant of his time with numerous miracles to his credit. His educational institution produced numerous scholars who went on to guide and serve the *ummah*. *Giyarwee* is the *esaal-e-thawaab* of the leader of saints *shaikh* Abdul Qadir Jilani.

The legitimacy of this practice is similar to the legitimacy of reading *khatam* for the deceased. The only difference is that rather than transferring blessings to him (we can think of them as gifts to him), we celebrate to attaining spiritual benefits.

38

Qs: Why do you decorate Mosques when Prophet Muhammad[S] has forbidden this?

Answer: Allah has not forbidden decorating Mosques (the best places on earth), except if this act distracts from one's compulsory duties.

Evidence from Holy Qur'an

"The mosques of Allah shall be maintained by those who believe in Allah and the last day." *(Holy Qur'an 9:18)*

Regarding this verse the commentators of the holy Qur'an state that performing prayers in congregation, keeping Mosques clean, spreading mats of high quality, brightening the Mosques with lighting etc. all this things are included in the prosperity of the Masjid. Or do we wish to pray in squalid conditions and see our donations not spent on decent decoration and beautification?

The key word in these verses is *'amara, ya'muru,* which implies the following: 1) to build or repair; 2) to maintain in fitting dignity; 3) to visit for purposes of devotion; and 4) to fill with light, life and activity. It is against this principle if Mosques are not enjoyed for their peace and serenity and this can only be undertaken in clean, decent and an attractive environment. Or is it that we wish our own homes to be beautiful but our places of worship unattractive?

Evidence from *Ahadith*

Hazrat Sulaiman[A] used to make the Masjid Baitul-Muqaddas bright with *Kibreet-e-Ahmar* (a flammable substance). There was so much brightness because of this that women miles away were able to spin their threads! – *(Roohul-Bayaan on HQ 9:18)*

Sayyidina Uthman[R] stated that the Messenger[S] of Allah said, 'If anyone builds a Mosque for Allah then Allah will build for him the like of it in Paradise.' *(Tirmithi 318, Ahmad 434, Bukhari 450, Muslim 533, Muwatta 736)*

It's clear that by building beautiful Mosques we are meant to attract worshippers and for this a person can get huge rewards. Islam only prohibits extravagant mosque beautification and decoration which diverts and distracts people from focusing on prayer as stated in the *ahadith* below:

Bukhari said: "'Umar said: 'Build for the people a place to worship Allah, and beware of using red or yellow for adornment and decoration and distracting the people thereby." *(Fathul Bari 1,642)*

Sayyidah Maimuna[R] asked the holy prophet[S] "give us instructions regarding the *Masjid* at *Baitul-muqaddas*", he said, "go to it and read *salah* there." During those times, there was war in that place. For this reason the holy prophet[S] said, "If you cannot reach the Masjid to perform salah in it, send oil there so that it can be used to light the Masjid lamps. *(Abu Daood 34:3)*

So, nice lighting (beautifying) and advertising the Mosque with lights is totally permissible.

Hazrat Abu Ishaq hamdaan states that on the first night of Ramadan, *hazrat* Ali[R] came to Masjid *Nabawi* while lamps were shinning and the recitation of the holy Qur'an was in progress, he said, "O 'Umar ibn Khattab[R] may Allah brighten your grave just as you have brightened his Masjid at the time of Qur'ans recitation *(Minhaj-us-sunnah vol2 p224)*

...Allah decorates his paradise every day (in Ramadan) and says, 'soon my pious worshippers shall set aside their trials and come to you'..*(Ahmad 8,136)*

Allah[swt] decorates His paradise and does it really follow that he wants his Mosques on the earth to be squalid, ugly and dull?

Discussion

Mosque decoration is not prohibited (*haram*). The most that has been said about mosque decoration is that it shouldn't interfere with people's concentration in prayers and in other worship activities.

We decorate the *Ka'bah* with beautiful cloth, the *haramain* we wish to make attractive and honourable, we decorate the blessed tomb of our beloved Prophet Muhammad[S] with beautiful verses of the Holy Qur'an and beautiful gates. Or should we not honour places of respect and worship? Allah[swt] is beautiful and loves beauty.

39

Qs: You have introduced names like *sufi, haji, wali, peer, shaikh* when these didn't exist at the time of Prophet Muhammad[S].

Answer: Introducing good titles for people is proven from Qur'an and *sunnah* and bad tittles are forbidden.

Evidence from Holy Qur'an

"And do not insult one another and do not call each other by (offensive) nicknames. Wretched is the name of disobedience after (one's) faith. *(Holy Qur'an 49:11)*

Allah[swt] commands us not to introduce inappropriate names for one another. It is a sin to call others by offensive or derogatory nicknames; or nicknames which are derived out of hatred, mockery, sarcasm, envy, jealousy, etc. But there is absolutely no harm in assigning or calling another by a good 'nickname', one which has been derived out of love and compassion.

For example, The Lord Most High has Himself assigned honourable names' for His Noble and Beloved Messenger[S] like *Muzammil* and *Mudatthir (Holy Qur'an 73:1 and 74:1)* meaning one who is wrapped up in a cloth or blanket; or the name Prophet Muhammad[S] assigned to his beloved cousin and son-in-law, *hazrat* Imam Ali[R] by calling him Abu-Turab (literally meaning 'father of dust' or 'one who lies upon dust')

Allah[swt] also lists in the Holy Qur'an titles for humans such as *Nabi, Rasool, Ansaar, Muhajiroon, Muslim, Mu'min, shuhadaa, siddiqeen, saaliheen, muttaqeen, awliyaa, 'ulemaa, Muhsineen, Imam* [20] to mention but a few.

Evidence from *Ahadith*

Narrated by Sahl bin Sad[R]. The most beloved names to Ali ibn Abi Talib[R] was '*Abu Turab*', and he used to be pleased when we called him by it, for no-one named him *Abu Turab* (for the first time), but the Prophet[S]. Once Ali got angry with (his wife) Fatimah, and went out (of his house) and slept near a wall in the mosque. The Prophet[S] came

searching for him, and someone said, 'He is there, lying near the wall.'
The Prophet[S] came to 'Ali while his ('Ali's) back was covered with
dust. The Prophet[S] started removing the dust, saying, 'Get up, O *Abu
Turab*! Get up, O *Abu Turab*!' *(Bukhari 8:233)*

The holy Prophet[S] gave a title to *hazrat* Ali[R] and this title became
so beloved to him. It was always the nature of the holy Prophet[S] to
address his companions with good names.

Narrated Abu Jubayrah ibn ad-Dahhak[R]: This verse was revealed
about us, the *Banu* Salimah: 'Nor call each other by (offensive)
nicknames: ill-seeming is a name connoting wickedness (to be used of
one) after he has believed.' He said: 'When the apostle of Allah came
to us, every one of us had two or three names. The Apostle[S] of Allah
began to say: 'O so and so! But they would say: Keep silence, Apostle
of Allah! He becomes angry by this name. So this verse was revealed:
"Nor call each other by (offensive nicknames.)" *(Abu Daood 4,944)*

Therefore, it is clearly permissible to call people by honourable
names or titles, not offensive ones.

Discussion

The titles and names that the scholars bestow on some of them, or
that the people bestow on them, are only referring to the level of
knowledge that a person acquires of the rulings of *Shari'ah*. There
may also be a kind of distinguishing the type of knowledge in
which a person has specialized, such as *faqeeh* or *mufti* for those
who have specialized in *fiqh* and issuing *fataawa*, respectively, or
mufassir for the one who has specialized in *tafseer* or commentary
on the Book of Allah. *Muhaddith* for those who have specialized in
the study of *hadith* and *hafiz* for the one who has memorised the
Holy Qur'an.

We use 'Doctor', 'Mr', 'Miss', 'Mrs', 'Ms', 'Professor', which is
not disputed, but to use similar terms for Islamic identification,
suddenly becomes forbidden? Thus, titles such as *sufi, peer hajji
wali, shaikh* are not bad titles to give to any Muslim as long as the
intention is correct as this in line with the *sunnah* of Allah[swt] and of
his beloved Prophet Muhammad[S]. Which it is.

40   Qs: Where is the proof of *shabbe barat*?

Answer: *Shabbe-barat* (15th *Sha'ban*) It is proven from Holy Qur'an and *hadith*.

Evidence from Holy Qur'an

"By the book that makes things clear, we sent it down during a blessed night, for we ever wish to warn against evil. In that night is made distinct every affair of wisdom." *(Holy Qur'an 44:1-5)*

In regards to this verse *Hazrat Akramah*[RA] and many *Mufassiroon* are of the opinion that this verse refers to the 15th of *Sha'ban*. In *Ruhool Maani* a narration of *hazrat ibn Abbas*[R]; wealth, life and death are written on the night of the 15th of *Sha'baan* and passed to the angels on the night of power *(laitul Qadr)*. *(Tafsir ibn kathir, ma'riful Qur'an vol.7 p758)*.

In *Tafsir* 'Uthman it is written that the 15th *Sha'ban* is when wealth, life and death of individuals are written and on the night of power *(Lailatul Qadr)* the matter is fulfilled.

Evidence from *Ahadith*

Ummul Mu'mineen Aishah[R] narrates: 'One night Rasulallah[S] was staying in my house, I did not find him at home. I left my house in search for him and found him at *Jannatul Baqi*. The Prophet[S] said: 'Aisha, did you feel that Allah and His Prophet would wrong you?' I *('Aisha)* then said: 'O *RasoolAllah*, I thought that you had gone to another of your wives.' He said, 'Allah turns His special attention towards the 1st Heaven on this night and forgives the number of His servants as much as are on the hairs on the sheep of *Bani Kalb.'* *(Tirmithi 739, Ahmad 26,077, Muwatta 14,389)*

Sayyidina Ali[A] narrates Rasoolullah[S] said: 'When the 15th night of *Sha'ban* comes, on that night busy yourself in worship and keep a fast during the day, for in that night, soon after sunset, the special mercy of Allah descends to the first Heaven and He proclaims, 'Is there any servant of Mine who begs forgiveness from Me that I may forgive him? Is there a servant of Mine who begs sustenance from Me that I may grant him sustenance? Is there a servant of mine in distress who asks for good health and well-being from Me that I may bestow good health and well-being upon him?' In the same manner, Allah calls different kinds of needy people to supplicate to Him for their needs at that time so that he may grant their supplications until the daybreak.' *(Ibn Majah 1,388, Targheeb 1,521)*

Hazrat Ayesh[R] relates, 'The Prophet[S] returned home and began to perform *Salah*. He fell into *sajdah* and performed such a long *sajdah* that I had feared he had passed away. When I saw this, I moved from my bed and moved his thumb. The thumb moved and I returned to my place. When the Prophet[S] had finished *Salah* he stated: '*Jibrail* came to me and said that <u>tonight is the middle night of *Sha'ban* (15th) and in this night Allah will forgive so many people from the Hellfire, as much as are the hairs on the sheep of *Bani Kalb*</u>. However, there are certain unfortunate individuals who will not be forgiven, even in this night. Those who join partners with Allah, those who have enmity for their brothers, those who break the ties of kith and kin, those men who keep their lower garment below their ankles (out of pride), those who disobey their parents and those who habitually drink alcohol.
(Baihaqqi 3,835 & 1,518, Targheeb 4,084 & 4,079

Sayyidina Mu'adh ibn Jabal reports that Rasoolullah[S] has said, 'Allah looks upon His creation in the middle night of *Sha'ban* and forgives all, except the one who associates partners with Him or the one who has malice in his heart (against a Muslim)".
(Baihaqqi – Shu'bal Iman, Targheeb 4,078 & 1,517)

These *ahadith* clearly indicate that 15th *Sah'ban* is blessed with enormous forgiveness and that we should pray and fast on that day.

Discussion

The night of the 15th *Sha'ban*, is a very blessed that has been observed by the holy prophet[S] himself and his companions[R] and the *ummah* for centuries. Allah[swt] turns towards His servants, fulfils their supplications for forgiveness and sustenance and fulfils the requests of the callers in this night. We should worship, supplicate and fast sincerely to attain maximum benefit.

With so many narrations proving the virtues of this night it is a tremendous blessing upon us. Denying such a blessed night is foolhardy and beyond wisdom.

81

Appendix 1

Common Misconceptions Clarified

In this section we clear up the common accusations made by ignorant people levied against our beloved Prophet Muhammad[S]. We don't know why people insist on trying to create confusion and their wish to insult him but that is for them to answer for. The following are answered here:

    1a Could the holy Prophet[S] read and write.

    1b Did the holy Prophet[S] forget things?

    1c Was the holy Prophet[S] misguided before announcement of prophet-hood.

    1d Did the blessed Prophet[S] make mistakes?

    1e Was the blessed heart of the Prophet[S] weak?

    1f Should we only accept ahadith from *Sahih Sitta*?

    1g Is the universe made from light of Prophet Muhammad[S]

    1h Why do people use numbers to replace words?

1a   Could the holy Prophet[S] read and write?

The Arabic word *ummi*, translated sometimes as as 'illiterate', does not mean illiterate, but rather means 'one who has no book', or those who did not have a book revealed by Allah[swt] *(Holy Qur'an 62:2)*. Thus, the Holy Qur'an was revealed, not to an illiterate prophet, but to a people who did not have their own book revealed by Allah[swt]. There is evidence from many ahadith of the holy Prophet[S] to prove this point.

Narrated Anas bin Malik: 'Once the Prophet[S] wrote a letter or had an idea of writing a letter. The Prophet[S] was told that they (rulers) would not read letters unless they were sealed. So the Prophet[S] got a silver ring made with "Muhammad Allah's Apostle" engraved on it. As if I

82

were just observing its white glitter in the hand of the prophet.
(Bukhari 3:863)

Thus, the beloved Prophet Muhammad[S] wished to write a letter, proving that he could write.

> Narrated 'Ubaidullah bin 'Abdullah: Ibn 'Abbas said, When the ailment of the prophet became worse, he said, 'Bring for me (writing) paper and <u>I will write for you a statement</u> after which you will not go astray.' But 'Umar[R] said, 'The prophet is seriously ill, and we have got Allah's Book with us and that is sufficient for us.' But the companions of the prophet differed about this and there was a hue and cry. On that the Prophet[S] said to them, 'Go away (and leave me alone). It is not right that you should quarrel in front of me.' Ibn 'Abbas came out saying, 'It was most unfortunate (a great disaster) that Allah's Apostle was prevented from writing that statement for them because of their disagreement and noise'. *(Bukhari 3:114)*

Again, it is clear that the Prophet Muhammad[S] offered to write something but declined due to the disagreement in front of him.

It is clear from the above evidence that the holy Prophet[S] could read and write but never demonstrated it out of his humility, out of his obedience to Allah[swt], and so that people would not be able to find a shred of evidence accusing him of writing the Holy Qur'an. To state that he couldn't read or write goes against his own sayings and against the Holy Qur'an.

When Jibraeel[A] asked the Prophet[S] to 'read' *(Bukhari 3)*, the reply was *'maa ana bi qaari'*. The literal meaning of this is 'I am not a reader'. In Arabic grammar, the word *qari* (in its genitive state, or *qari'un* in its nominative state) is a derivative noun in the form of the 'active present participle' *(ism al-fa'il)*, and hence – etymologically speaking – it can have the meaning of the imperfect tense *(al-fi'l al-mudari')*. In this case, the aforementioned phrase would mean 'I do not read' or 'I will not read'.

Based upon this, the phrase *'maa ana bi qaari'* has three possible meanings: 'I am not a reader', 'I do not read' and 'I will not read'. In reality, as Jibraeel[A] was asking the Prophet Muhammad[S] to 'read' without beginning in the name of Allah, the Prophet[S], declined until Allah's name was mentioned. The embrace was Jibraeel[A] gaining spirituality from Prophet Muhammad[S]. The shivering of the Prophet's[S] body was not due to weakness, but a reaction as the words of Allah were being imprinted on his blessed heart. Allah[swt] himself says that His creation cannot take such power of the Holy Qur'an and the mountains would be destroyed if they would receive such words revealed upon them *(HQ 59:21)*.

1b   Did the holy Prophet[S] forget things?

"By degrees shall we teach thee (O Muhammad[S]) to declare (the message), so thou shall not forget, except as God wills." *(Holy Qur'an 87:6-7)*

This verse is not saying that Prophet Muhammad[S] forgets because of any weakness. It is saying that he will only forget if God wills and this is enough evidence to prove his perfection. In other words, sometimes Allah[swt] makes him forget for our guidance, not to show he has imperfection. To then say the beloved Prophet Muhammad[S] forgets because he is weak, is an insult to Allah[swt] as Allah[swt] is saying He makes him forget and Allah[swt] is not certainly not weak.

It is reported by Bashar on the authority of Yazid on the authority of Sa'eed, that Qatada said that Prophet Muhammad[S] never forgot anything (except as God willed). Commenting on this verse the meaning of this statement, 'Thou shall not forget', except as God wills what you should forget and don't remember it, they said: That is what Allah has abrogated from the Qur'an, so he lifted its wisdom and recitation. *(Ibn Jarir al-Tabari, Jami' al-bayan fi ta'wil al-Qur'an, Commentary on Holy Qur'an 87:7)*

"Your companion does not make errors nor does he deviate" *(Holy Qur'an 53:2)*

Allah[swt] is clear about this point. The blessed Prophet[S] does not make errors and does not deviate from the truth, so any accusation against him in this way is baseless and pointless.

1c   Was the holy Prophet^S misguided before announcement of prophet-hood?

"And we found Thee lost (in love and worship), so guided thee
(through that worship)" *(Holy Qur'an 93:7)*

The above verse is sometimes misunderstood and even mistranslated as: "We found you 'misguided' so guided you". This is absolutely false and totally incorrect. Allah^{swt} says as already quoted previously:

"Your companion does not make errors nor does he deviate" *(Holy Qur'an 53:2)*

Thus, the correct translation should be that Allah^{swt} found the beloved Prophet^S lost in his worship, and He showed the way to an even deeper worship. It is necessary to point out here that the explanation given to the verse *'Wa wajadka daallan fa hadaa'* by some of our 'misguided scholars' to say it indicates that the holy Prophet^S was somehow in error and then was guided. This is completely wrong.

It is true that *'daallan'* can mean *'on the wrong path'*, but that is not the only meaning. It also signifies *'wandering in search of'* and *'lost in love for'*, as the Holy Qur'an itself says in relation to the Prophet Ya'qoub^A: *Innaka fi dalalatikal qadeem* *(Holy Qur'an 12:95)* - You are still lost in your old infatuation). Here, the reference is to the Prophet Ya'qoub's great love for his son, Prophet Yusuf^A. Similarly, we find the expression in the Arabic language: *Daallal ma'u fil labani* (The water is lost in the milk – not the water is misguided!).

However, one can still question why we felt obliged to reject the meaning of *daallan* here as *'on the wrong path'*, and select the other two meanings above.

As already explained, The Holy Qur'an states *Maa dalla saahibukum wa maa ghawaa* 'Your companion (i.e. the Holy Prophet) does not make error nor does he deviate' *(HQ 53:2)*.

The Holy Prophet^S lived day and night before the eyes of his people and committed no error. How can that same book contradict itself by asserting: '*You* (the Holy Prophet) *were going astray*' (wrongly guided) *and then We guided thee* (to the right path)?' Are we then saying that Allah[swt] misguided him first? Are we saying that Allah[swt] did not create him properly as a Messenger? This explanation is totally erroneous and completely untrue. The true significance of this verse is:

"You were wandering in search of Me or you were lost in love for Me so I guided you to your desired destination."

Thus we are given a beautiful insight into how Allah[swt] took great care and gave great attention to Prophet Muhammad[S]. It also shows us how classified, close and powerful the bond is between the Creator and the greatest of His creation and how deep in worship our beloved Prophet[S] is. The various dimensions and depth of this worship we can never fathom or fully understand as it is as personal as it is wondrous.

"And we found Thee lost (in love and worship), so guided thee (through that worship)" *(Holy Qur'an 93:7)*

In addition, he was known by all as *Al-Ameen* & *As-Saadiq* (the trustworthy & truthful) before he announced his prophet-hood.

1d   Did the blessed Prophet[S] make mistakes?

The answer is simply no. (Please also see chapter 20.) He does not and has never made mistakes. In order to try and convince the public, some people try and use the following hadith in a vain attempt to prove otherwise:

Narrated from Râfi` b. Khurayj: The Prophet[S] had come to Madinah while they were cross-pollinating their date palms. He asked, 'What are these people doing?' They replied, 'This is something that has been our practice.' He said, 'Maybe if you were not to do so, it would be good.' So they abandoned it and the crop that resulted was impoverished. They mentioned this to him and he said, 'I am only a human being. When I command you with something regarding your religion, accept it. When I command you with something from my own opinion, then I am only a human being." `Ikrimah (one of the hadith's narrators) said: "He said that or something to that effect."
(Muslim 2,362)

Imam Nawawi[R] states the following about this narration:

'The phrase 'from my own opinion' is only brought by Ikrimah as a narration by meaning. This is because Ikrimah says at the end of the hadith, '...or something to that effect." *(Sharh Sahih Muslim 15:116)*

Muslim mentions the narration of Anas last. This narration comes to us by way of a chain of transmission that includes the narrator Hammad bin Salamah, and Hammad was prone to make mistakes. This is the only narration of the story that contains the statement: "You know best the affairs of your worldly life."

Thus, the words of the Prophet[S] as quoted here are not sufficiently reliable to be accepted as fact – especially as they disagree with the holy Qur'an:

"Nay! By your Lord! They will not believe until they make you the judge in their disputes among themselves and then find within themselves no difficulty in what you decide, and submit to it in full submission." *(Holy Qur'an 3:65)*

"Indeed We have sent down to you (O Muhammad) the Book in truth so you may judge between the people by that which Allah has shown you and not be an advocate for the deceitful." *(Holy Qur'an 4:105)*

Thus, the Prophet Muhammad[S] has absolute authority, should not be disagreed with, nor can he make mistakes. In reality, it is likely that he indicated that matters of worship are separated from matters of domestic concern. It is also feasible that he never indicated to the people to abandon the practice but they misunderstood him as a result of which the crops became impoverished. Further:

"Whoever obeys the messenger, indeed he has indeed obeyed Allah."
(Holy Qur'an 4:80)

How can Allah[swt] allow this if the blessed Prophet[S] made mistakes?

1e   Was the blessed heart of the Prophet[S] weak?

"Did we not expand your breast" *(Holy Qur'an 97:1)*

There are famous accounts of Jibraeel[A] coming down and opening the blessed heart and removing a small, black piece of meat. Some ignorant people regard this as being a weakness in the blessed heart of Prophet Muhammad^S. This is not the case as Allah^{swt} says:

"And we did not send you except as a mercy to the entire universe"
(Holy Qur'an 21:107)

Therefore, the blessed heart of the Prophet Muhammad^S, touches every part of the universe as this is the seat of his blessed mercy. Even Satan the outcast received this mercy but Allah^{swt} decreed that the blessed mercy of Prophet Muhammad^S should not be connected to *Iblees*. Therefore, Jibraeel^A performed open heart surgery and removed that very small and particular part of the heart.

Why should the Angel Jibraeel^A require to wash the blessed heart and chest of Prophet Muhammad^S? Again, some attempt to say that it required washing due to the connection of mercy to Iblees, and what better way of washing than to use the greatest of waters – the waters of paradise. However, Allah^{swt} states that he expanded his blessed chest *(HQ 97:1)*. Therefore, it can only mean that the waters of paradise required the blessing from the blessed heart of Prophet Muhammad^S. After all, were these waters not created out of his *noor* in the first place? So why did his blessed heart and chest require washing? No. The waters of paradise are now so blessed as they have had physical contact with the blessed heart and seat of the mercy to the universe. *Subhanallah.*

1f   Should we only accept *ahadith* from *Sahih Sitta*?

Sahih Sitta is a term referring to the 6 books of Bukhari, Muslim, Ibne Maja, Abu Daood, Tirmithi and Nisaai. There are many *ahadith* in these collections that are *sahih* (authentic) but this doesn't mean that there are no other ahadith that are *sahih*. The mission of the various collators was not to collect every single *sahih hadith* in existence but the collators wanted a concise, useful and authentic reference book for Muslims on a variety of topics but not all topics. Also, not all the *ahadith* quoted in these are *sahih*.

Sahih is used in the classification of *hadith* and signifies a level of authenticity. There are other levels of authenticity as well such as

Hassan for example which are also unanimously accepted. Just because a *hadith* is classified as 'weak' doesn't mean it's made up or fabricated. It's a level of classification. Many other authentic collections exist - as referred to in Appendix 2 - collated by great scholars and *Muhaditheen* which are used extensively by scholars. It is easy to dismiss these if one is not sincere in seeking the truth. We would suggest that sincerity demand these to be looked at.

1g Is the universe made from light of Prophet Muhammad[S]

It is related that Jabir ibn `Abd Allah said to the Prophet[S]: 'O Messenger of Allah, may my father and mother be sacrificed for you, tell me of the first thing Allah created before all things.' He said, 'O Jabir, the first thing Allah created was the light of your Prophet from His light, and that light remained (literally 'turned') in the midst of His Power for as long as He wished, and there was not, at that time, a Tablet or a Pen or a Paradise or a Fire or an angel or a heaven or an earth. No sun, no moon, no Jinn, no human.

And when Allah wished to create creation, he divided that Light into four parts and from the first made the Pen, from the second the Tablet, from the third the Throne. The fourth part He divided into 4 parts. He created holders of the throne from the first part, the Chair from the second and the rest of the Angels form the 3rd. He then divided the 4th part into 4 parts. He created the heavens from the first, the earth form the second, the paradise and hell form the third. Then He divided the 4th into 4 parts.

So he created the light of vision of the believers from the 1st, the light of their hearts form the second and it is recognition of Allah. Light of their love from the 3rd and the 4th *Tawheed.*

(Qastalani in Mawahib ul Laduniyah Volume 1, Page No. 71 & [21]

Clearly, Allah[swt] utilised His light as 'raw material' to create the light of our beloved Prophet Muhammad[S] without using or diminishing any of His light. Allah[swt] didn't need to use anything but He chose to do it this way, such that there would be a close connection between Him and the greatest of His creation. The table below summarises the mathematical proportions of this division:

1/4	1/4	1/4	
Pen	Tablet	Throne	
1/16	1/16	1/16	
Holders of the Throne	Chair	Angels	
1/64	1/64	1/64	
Heavens	Earth	Paradise & Hell	
1/256	1/256	1/256	1/256
Light of vision of believers	Light of heart of the believers	Light of love of the believers	Kalimah Tayyibah

1h   Why do People use Numbers to Replace Words?

The letters of the Arabic Alphabet in numerical order									
ا	ب	ج	د	ه	و	ز	ح	ط	
1	2	3	4	5	6	7	8	9	
ي	ك	ل	م	ن	س	ع	ف	ص	
10	20	30	40	50	60	70	80	90	
ق	ر	ش	ت	ث	خ	ذ	ض	ظ	غ
100	200	300	400	500	600	700	800	900	1000

As we do not wish to insult Allah's words, so we replace Qur'anic phrases with numbers. This is to prevent papers with verses of Holy Qur'an from being thrown away. So if we add up the numbers associated with the letters in *tasmiyyah*, we would get 786. The name Muhammad[S] is 92. Throwing numbers away is permissible but we shouldn't throw away Qur'anic words in the bin.

Appendix 2

Summary of Books Referenced

1. Musnad Ahmad ibn Hanbal

Collection of Ahadith - *compiled by Imam Ahmad bin Muhammad bin Hambal Aby 'Abdul A'laa ash-shaybani (known as Imam Ahmad bin Hambal). (164 – 241 AH, 780 – 855 CE) 28,414 ahadith in 11 volumes)*

Imam Ahmad being very fond of *sunnah* started a collection of *ahadith* at the early age of sixteen. This *Musnad* contains over 28,000 *ahadith* selected from over 700,000 collected by him and over 100,000 memorised by him. He was so strict about the selection of authentic *ahadith* that the process of scrutiny continued till he breathed his last. Imam Abu Daood said of his gatherings, '...they were the gatherings of the afterlife...'. The last of the great *Mujtahid* Imams, he was imprisoned and tortured for 28 months but refused to denounce the fact that the Holy Qur'an is the uncreated word of Allah[swt]. It is said that many tens of thousands attended his funeral procession. He never missed praying at night time and it is even the case that Almighty Allah came to him in a dream.

It is said that his *Musnad* is the greatest collection of *ahadith*. It is also said that this *Musnad* is as or more authentic and reliable as compared to other *Musaneed*. Some have said that this book equals Sunnan Abu Daood and Jami' Tirmithi.

2. *Sahih* Al-Bukhari

Collection of Ahadith - *compiled by Abu 'Abdullah Muhammad bin Ismaeel bin Ibraheem bin al Mugheera bin Bardizba al Jufi al Bukhari (known as Imam Bukhari). (194 - 256 AH, 816-878 CE, 7,563 ahadith)*

This book is considered to be the most authentic book after the Holy Qur'an. However, this is through its fame rather than correctness. The compiler thereof is Muhammad Ismail of Bukhara[R], commonly known as Imam Bukhari. *(194-256 AH, 816-878 CE)*. He was raised as an orphan and travelled and gathered 600,000 *ahadith*. Imam Bukhari[R] had written several books, but his most distinguished work was this compilation of *ahadith* titled as ' *al Jaama'e al Saheeh Al Musnad min Hadith Rasool Allah*^{S} *wa Sunnahi wa Ayyamihi'*.

Imam Bukhari was inspired by his most beloved teacher *Imam Ishaq ibn Rahwayh (161 – 238 AH)*, who was a *muhaddith, faqih*, and the Imam of Khurasan of his time, Thus he compiled a book that contains only *Saheeh ahadith* - those that fulfilled all the criterion of soundness and reliability of *isnad* (chain of narration) and *matan* (text). From the collected *ahadith*, Imam Bukhari had inferred the biography of *rasoolullah*^{S} and the principles of *fiqh* (jurisprudence).

This book is divided into 97 chapters, that are further subdivided into 3,450 chapters. In total this book contains over 7,000 ahadith. If the repeated *ahadith* are omitted then the number falls down to 4,000. Detailed commentaries and *Sharh* (explanations) have been written for this 'Saheeh al-Bukhari', the most prominent one is that of Hafiz ibn Hajar Assqalani, titled as ' *Fath al-Bari'*.

Sahih al-Bukhari was completed and published by his students as the great imam passed away before being able to publish the collection although it had been mostly compiled.

3.   *Sahih* Muslim

Collection of Ahadith - *compiled by Abu al Husain Asakir ad-deen bin Al-Hajjaj bin Muslim bin Ward bin kawshath al Qushair an-Naysabur (known as Imam Muslim) (202-261 AH, 824 – 883 CE, 7,190 ahadith).*

It is the known (through fame) as the second most authentic hadith collection after Sahih Al-Bukhari, and is highly acclaimed book. This was compiled by Muslim bin Al-Hajjaj who was a native of Neshapur in Khorasan *(202-261 AH, 824 – 883 CE)*.

Out of 300,000 hadith which he evaluated, approximately 7,000 were extracted for inclusion into his collection based on stringent acceptance criteria. Each report in his collection was checked and the veracity of the chain of reporters was painstakingly established. Muslim is divided into 43 books.

It is estimated that there are a total of 4,000 a*hadith* (without repetition). In this *Sahih* and Imam Muslim collected those *ahadith* which are narrated by at least two narrators of all the periods right from him to that of the Prophet[S]. For Imam Muslim all the narrators had not only to be honest but they had to fulfil all the conditions of being a witness. In this book 218 *Sahaaba ikraam* (companions) are included as narrators, whereas in Sahih al-Bukhari this number is 208.

A large number of commentaries and *Sharih* (explanations) have been written for *Sahih* Muslim. These include *Al-Dibaj ela Sahih Muslim* by Imam Jalaluddin Suyuti or *Sharah Muslim* by Mulla Ali Qari. The creditability of this *Sahih* can be judged by the opinion of some of the scholars who rate this book over Saheeh Bukhari.

4. *Sunan* Abu Daood

Collection of Ahadith - compiled by *Abu Daood bin Sulaiman bin al-Asha'as al Azdi al as-sijistani, (known as Abu Daud) (202-275 AH, 824-897 CE, 5,769 ahadith).*

This is the most distinguished work of Imam Abu Dawood. *Sunan* Abu Daud was compiled by Sulaiman bin Al-Ashah, known as Abu Daud *(202-275 AH, 824-897 CE)*. Some of the scholars have graded this book after *Sahih* al-Bukhari and *Sahih* Muslim.

It was also narrated that Abu Dawood said: "I wrote 500,000 *ahadeeth* on the authority of the Messenger of Allah[S], I selected from them what I included in this book – meaning '*Sunan Abu Dawood*' – I collected 4,800 *ahadeeth* in it.

In his book *Sunan*, Abu Dawood also stated: 'I examined the *ahadeeth* on the authority of the Messenger and found they were (approximately) four thousand *Ahadeeth*, I further examined them and found that these four thousand revolve around four (titles):

(1) An Nu'maan ibn Basheer's *hadeeth:* "What is permissible is clear and what is forbidden is clear..."

(2). 'Umar's *hadith*: "Indeed actions are only based on intentions..."

(3) Abu Hurayrah's *hadith*: "Indeed Allah is good and does not accept anything except good, and Allah ordered the believers with the same things he ordered the messengers…"

(4) Abu Hurayrah's *hadith*: "From the proficiency of a person's Islam, is to leave off what does not concern him."

He then stated: 'Each of these four *ahadith* is a quarter of knowledge.'

5.   *Sunan* al- Tirmithi

Collection of Ahadith - *compiled by Abu 'Isa Muhammad bin 'Isa as-Sulamu ad-Darir al-Bughi at-Tirmithi (known as Imam Tirmithi). (210 – 279 AH, 824– 892 CE, 3,956 ahadith)*

Like others, Imam Tirmithi also wrote several books, but the most outstanding of those is *Sunan* al-Tirmithi, also called as al- Jami. Tirmithi, by Abu Muhammad bin `Isa bin Surah. He named his book Sunan al-Tirmithi. He offers much information on *usul al-hadith* and methodology of *hadith* transmission.

Having grown up in an environment of learning, together with possessing many great qualities naturally drove Imam Tirmithi to dedicate his life totally towards the field of *hadith*. He obtained his basic knowledge at home and later travelled to far off lands in search of this great science.   He studied *hadith* under great personalities such as Imam Bukhari, Imam Muslim and Imam Abu Daood. In some narrations Imam Bukhari and Imam Muslim are his students as well.   According to Ibn Taymiyya and Shah Waliullah, Imam Tirmithi was an independent Jurist (*Mujtahid*). *Maulana* Anwar Shah Kashmiri is of the opinion that he was a *Shafi`i.*

Before Imam Tirmithi, Imam Daood Tayalisi and Imam Ahmed ibn Hanbal had compiled books that contains both authentic and weak ahadith. Later Imam Bukhari compiled his Saheeh and omitted all weak narrations from it. His main objective was to derive *masa'il* (laws) from the relevant *ahadith*. Later Imam Muslim compiled his book with a primary focus on the *'isnad'* (chain of narrators). Imam Nasa'i's aim was to mention the discrepancies of the hadith whilst Abu Dawud prepared a book which became the basis for the *'fuqaha'* (jurisprudists).

Imam Tirmithi had combined the styles of Bukhari, Muslim, Abu Daood and Nisaai by mentioning the discrepancies regarding the narrators and also making his compilation a basis for the jurists. The Special characteristics of *al-Jami`ut-Tirmithii)* is that it is a *'Sunan'* and a *'Jami`i)*. Only 83 ahadith are repeated.

Imam Tirmithi omits the major portion of the *ahadith* and only mentions that part which is relevant to the heading. After mentioning a *hadith* he classifies it narration (whether it is authentic or weak, etc.). He specifies the narrators names in full along with *kunya* (agnomen or nick-name). One hadith in *Tirmithi* is a *thulaathiyaat* i.e. the transmitters of the hadith between Imam Tirmithi and the Prophet (s) are only three. He gives an explanation to all difficult ahadith and there is no fabricated hadith in the entire book. Several commentaries have been written for Jami' al-Tirmithi, like Qut-ul Mughtazi, compiled by Allama Jalal ad-Din Suyuti.

6.   Sunan An-Nisaa'i

Collection of Ahadith - compiled by Hafiz Abu `Abdur Rahman Ahmad bin Shu`ayb bin Ali bin Sinan an-Nasaai (known as Imam Nasaai). (214 – 303 AH, 829 – 915 CE, 5,769 ahadith)

Imam Ahmad Abu Abdur Rahman An-Nisaa'i wrote several books, but his collection of *ahadith* has an outstanding position. Nisaa'i, was Hafiz Abu `Abdur Rahman Ahmad bin Shu`ayb. He named his book Sunan al-Nisaai. The initial collection of *ahadith* was named *Sunan Kubra*, that contained both *sahih* and *hassan ahadith*. On the demand of the ruler of his time he compiled another book that contained only *sahih ahadith* and named it as ' *Al-Mutaba'* or *Sunan al-Sagheer* or *Sunan an-Nasa'ii*.

An-Nisaai contains 5,270 *ahadith* including the repeated ones. The criterion of selection of *ahadith* was much stricter than Imam Bukhari and Muslim, but a good number of weak *ahadith* are included in this book. Several commentaries and *Sharuh* (explanations) have been written on *Sunan An-Nasa'ii*, including '*Dhuhar al-Reba ilal Mujtaba*' by Hafiz Jalaluddin Suyuti.

7.   Sunan ibn Majah

Collection of Ahadith - compiled by Abu 'Abdillah Muhamamd bin Yazid, bin Majah ar-Rabi'i al Qazwin (known as ibn Majah). (209 – 273 AH, 824- 887 CE, 4,397 ahadith)

Muhammad Abdullah ibn Majah had three well known books to his credit and out of these Sunan ibn Majah has the most distinguished position. Ibn Majah was Abu Abdullah Muhammad bin Yazid al-Qizwini *(died 273 AH)*. He named his book Sunan Ibn Majah and it contains over 4,000 *ahadith* in 32 *abwaab* (chapters) divided into 1,500 sub-chapters.

Abu Zara'a Razi says, "I think that if this book reaches into the hands of the people then the other books will become irrelevant". This book is said to have about 30 *da'eef* (weak) *ahadith*. For this reason some scholars put question marks on this book. However, this books stands amongst the top most authentic books of *ahadith*. This book has an edge over other books with respect to its arrangement and non-repetition of *ahadith*. Also it has such unique *ahadith* that are not present in other top-most books. Several '*Sharuh*' (explanations) have been written for this book, including '*Sharah Sunan ibn Majah*' by Hafiz Alauddin Mughtalai *(died 762 AH)*.

9.   Sunan al-Daarimi

Collection of Ahadith - compiled by `Abd Allah bin `Abd al-Rahman al-Darimi (known as al-Darimi) (181 – 255 AH, 797 – 869 CE, 3,557 ahadith)

Imam Abdullah al- Darimi is a renowned *muhaddith*. *Sunan al-Darimi* is considered among the nine top most books of *ahadith*. This book of *ahadith* collected by Imam Darimi is known as 'al-Musnad' or *Sunan al-Darimi*. It consists of 1,508 *abwaab* (chapters) and 3,557 *ahadith*. *Muhaddithin* have acknowledged the creditability of this book as the reported weaknesses of the narrators are comparatively less and there are very few *munkir* (rejected) *ahadith* in it. Its authentic numbers of narrators *(isnad)* is high and number of *thalathiaat ahadith* (only 3 people in the chain) are more than in Sahih al-Bukhari.

10. Kanzul 'Umaal

Collection of Ahadith - compiled by Ali bin al Hussun-ud-deen al Muttaqi al-Hind (888 – 975 AH, 1472 – 1567 CE, 46,622 ahadith in 16 volumes)

Kanz al-'Ummal fi sunan al-aqwal wa'l af'al is an Islamic *hadith* collection, collected by the Islamic Scholar Ali ibn Abd-al-Malik al-Hindi. He collected from all of the major books. Ali al-Muttaqi's major work is Kanz al-'Ummal regarding which his teacher Abu al-Hasan al-Bakri al-Siddiqi says: " Al-Suyuti has done a great favour upon the entire world by writing al-Jami' al-Saghir and 'Ali al-Muttaqi has done a great service to al-Suyuti by compiling and arranging his work of al-Jami' al-Saghir"Al-Muttaqi was born 888 AH, CE 1472 in Burhanpur which is a town situated in modern day Southern Madhya Pardesh on the banks of the river Tapti, India.

'Ali al-Muttaqi writes in his autobiography that when he was eight years old, it occurred to him father to enrol him in the service of Shaykh Bajan. The Shaykh instructed him in sama'and Shaykh 'Abd al-Rahim Bajan taught me adhkar. 'Ali al- Muttaqi soon after earned his living as a scribe. He travelled to different regions of Hindustan and travelled to Multan to meet Shaykh Hisam al-Din al-Muttaqi and stayed under his guardianship, here he was instructed in Tasawwuf.

'Ali al-Muttaqi then travelled to Makkah and stayed in the company of Abu al-Hasan al-Bakri al-Siddiqi, from whom he acquired knowledge of *hadith* and Tasawwuf. 'Ali al- Muttaqi wrote some of his early works in Makkah. 'Ali al-Muttaqi also studied with the famous scholar of *hadith* Shaykh Shihab al-Din Ahmad bin Hajar al-Makki.

11.   Baihaqqi – Sunan al Kubra

Collection of Ahadith - compiled by Abu Bakr Ahmad bin Husaynbin 'Ali bin Musa al-Khosrojerdi al-Bayhaqi (known as Bayhaqi) (384 – 458 AH, 994- 1066 CE) (21,812 ahadith in 10 Volumes)

Abu Bakr Ahmad ibn Husayn Ibn 'Ali Ibn Moussa al-Khosrojerdi al-Baihaqqi, also known as Imam Al-Bayhaqqi was born 994 CE/384AH in the small town of Khusraugird near Sabzevar, then known as Bayhaq, in Khurasan. During his lifetime, he became a famous Sunni hadith expert. He was considered a learned Hafith among the eminent Imams of Hadith and a jurisprudence scholar in the Shafi'ee Madhab.

He wrote other books like As-Sunan Al-Kubra and As-Sunan As-Sughra. Adh-Dhahabi said, "His books exceed one thousand volumes." Al-Baihaqqi, which he is named after, is a town near Nishapur. Al-Baihaqqi died in 458 H. Sunan al-Kubra ("The Major Work") in about ten large volumes, concerning which Ibn al-Subki said: "No such book was ever compiled in the science with respect to classification, arrangement, and elegance. Thus book relates to the *sunnah* of the Prophet[S].

Among some of his work is Dala'il al-Nubuwwa (The Evidence of Prophet-hood) in seven volumes, the foremost large book exclusively devoted to the person of the Prophet[S] as al-Qadi 'Iyad's al-Shifa' fi Ma'rif Huquq al-Mustafa (The Healing concerning Knowledge of the Elect Prophet's Rights) is the foremost condensed book on this noble subject. Baihaqqi also collated another book on *hadith* called Shu'bal Iman which is also referenced.

12.   Mustadrak al Hakim

Collection of Ahadith - compiled by al Imam al Haafith Abullaahi al-Hakim al-Nishaburi (321 – 402, 933 – 1012 CE, 8,803 ahadith in 5 volumes)

Al-Mustadrak 'ala al-Sahihayn, is a five volume *hadith* collection written by Hakim al-Nishaburi. He wrote it in 1002–1003 CE, when he was 72 years old. It contains almost 9,000 *ahadith*. He claimed all *hadith* in it were authentic according to the conditions of either *Sahih* al-Bukhari or *Sahih* Muslim or both (hence the title *sahihayn*).

The Mustadrak contains a good number of *hadith* that conform to the conditions of authenticity of both (Bukhari and Muslim) as well as a number of *hadith* conforming to the conditions of either one of them. Perhaps the total number of such *hadith* comprises half the book

Mustadrak 'Alal Sahehayn, is one of the collections of *ahadith* that have been written by the great Hafith Imam Al Hakim, Al-Nisaburi. In this large work the imam tried to collect the *ahadith* that Imam Bukhari and Imam Muslim missed out in their respective known works. He tried to follow the method used by the above mentioned Imams in their respective *Saheeh*. Unfortunately he came short of that goal as it has been explain by works that followed later, such as those of Imam Al Dahabi in his famous works (Al-Talkhis, Al-Mizan) or that of Imam Al 'Iraqi (Imaaliya) or Imam Al Manawi (Faydhal Qader). They and others have detailed some narrations that did not meet the criteria of Imam Bukhari and Muslim.

13.   Mishkat al-Masabih

Collection of Ahadith - compiled originally by Abu Muhammad al-Hussain bin Mas'ood bin Muhammad al-Faraa al Baghwi (433 – 516 AH, 1042 - 1122 CE) and explanded upon by Muhammad bin 'Abd Allah Khatib Al-Tabrizi (died 741 AH)

Mishkaat al-Masaabih (a niche for lamps) is an expanded version of by Al-Baghawi's 'Masaabih al-Sunnah' by Muḥammad ibn 'Abd Allah Khatib Al-Tabrizi. Al-Tabrizi rendered the original version more accessible to those not having an advanced knowledge of the science of *hadith* and hence the complete name came about. It contains between 4,434 and 5,945 *ahadith*, divided into 29 books and is considered by Sunni scholars an important writing.

Al-Tabrizi added 1,511 *ahadith* to the original in the collection Masabih al-Sunnah. Al-Baghawi classified many *ahadith* as authentic when at times Al-Tabrizi did not agree. Al-Tabrizi expounded on the labels he placed on the *ahadith* and re-classified many of them. He added a third section to Masabih al-Sunnah, which was already divided in two parts by Al-Baghawi. Al-Baghawi did not mention the isnad of the *ahadith* he collected, so Al-Tabrizi mentions the source from where the hadith is originally found making the text more reliable.

14.   Al-Musannaf ibn shayba

Collection of Ahadith - *compiled by al-Imam 'Abd Allah bin Abi Shaybah bin Ibraheem 'Uthman bin Wassata Abu Bakr al-'Abbas (born 235 AH, 850 CE)*

Abu Bakr al-'Abasi is described by al-Dhahabi as the brother, father, and uncle of hadith masters and their most prestigious representative, 'the master of hadith masters...one of those who have reached the sky, an apex of trustworthiness. One of the oceans of knowledge. The author of al-Musnad, al-Ahkam, al-Musannaf, and al-Tafsir. One of the peers of Ahmad ibn Hanbal, Ishaq ibn Rahuyah, and 'Ali ibn al-Madini in age, place of birth, and hadith memorization.'

Abu Zur'a al-Razi said, 'I never saw anyone with more mastery of the hadith than Abu Bakr ibn Abi Shayba.' His scholarly relatives are: his brothers 'Uthman ibn Abi Shayba and al-Qasim ibn Abi Shayba; his son Ibrahim ibn Abi Bakr ibn Abi Shayba; and his nephew Abu Ja'far Muhammad ibn 'Uthman ibn Abi Shayba.

All are hadith masters except al-Qasim, who is weak. 'Abd Allah ibn Abi Shayba took *hadith* from Sharik ibn 'Abd Allah al-Qadi at age fourteen, Ibn al-Mubarak, Sufyan ibn 'Uyayna, Hushaym ibn Bashir, Waki' ibn al-Jarrah, Yahya al-Qattan, Isma'il ibn 'Iyash, Isma'il ibn 'Ulayya, and other major authorities. He took his selection from Bukhari and Muslim, Abu Dawud, Ibn Majah, Ahmad ibn Hanbal, Abu Zur'a, Ibn Abi 'Asim, Buqayy ibn Makhlad, al-Baghandi, Abu Ya'la al-Musili, Salih Jazara, 'Abdan, Abu al-Qasim al-Baghawi, and others.

15.   Al Adab al Mufrad

Collection of Ahadith - compiled by Abu 'Abdullah Muhammad bin Ismaeel bin Ibraheem bin al Mugheera bin Bardizba al Jufi al Bukhari (known as Imam Bukhari). (194 - 256 AH, 816-878 CE, 1,322 ahadith)

The Holy Prophet's[S] words are as relevant today as they were fourteen hundred years ago. This unique collection of 1,322 ahadith is one of the earliest and most authentic works on Islamic etiquette and the Islamic way of life. Not only are they practical and inspiring, but they also fulfil a desperate need for an authoritative guide on morality and spirituality for Muslims living in a modern, secular society where the line between right and wrong is increasingly blurred.

It provides a vivid insight into the moral conduct of the early Muslims in a society led by the perfect character of the Prophet, may Allah bless him and grant him peace, ('I was only sent to perfect good character'). The Companions represent excellent examples of men of vigorous moral stature whose conduct inspired and attracted masses to the fold of Islam wherever they went during the expansion of the Muslim territories, and contrary to the stereotypic portrayal, in the West, of Islam as being spread by the sword.

This book is an essential cornerstone of Islamic morality and is suitable for both the general reader and the academic alike. Its author, Imam Bukhari is one of the most celebrated figure in Islamic literary history.

16.   Al-Maqaasid al-Hasanah

Collection of Ahadith - compiled by Imam Shams-uddeen Muhammad 'Abd
al-Rahman al-Shawki   (831 – 902 AH, 1428 – 1497 CE)

Al-Maqasid al-Hasanah fi Bayan Kathir min al-Ahadith al-
Mushtaharat 'ala al-Alsinah authored by Imam Muhammad 'Abd al-
Rahman al-Sakhawi (d. 902).   One of the most popular and less
condensed works about prophetic narrations that are popular among
laymen. This was written for the purpose of clarifying the status or
the authenticity of above mentioned ahadith.   As it is an authentic
narration from the prophet[S] that mentions the position of an
individual who willingly attributes a lie to prophet.   Hence the need
for this work and others like it.

The Imam is an established authority on prophetic narrations. He
has organized the narrations according to their alphabetical order
and are, therefore, easier to locate.   Imam Shams-uddeen was a
reputable Shafi'i, *hadith* scholar and historian who was born in
Cairo. Al-Sakhawi refers to the village of Sakha in Egypt, where
his relatives belonged. He was a prolific writer that excelled in the
knowledge of *hadith, tafsir,* literature, and history. His proficiency
in *hadith* has its influences trace back heavily on his Shaykh: Al-
Hafidh Ibn Hajar al-'Asqalani. He died in Medina.

17.   As-Shifaah

Seerah - Authored by Al Imam al-Haafith Abul Fadal 'Iyad bin Musa bin
'Iyad al-Yahsabi (476 – 544 AH, 1083 – 1149 CE)

Kitab Ash-shifa bi-tarif huqub al-Mustafa also translated as
'Healing' by the recognition of the Rights of the Chosen One of
Qadi Iyad is perhaps the most frequently used and most commented
upon handbook in which the Prophet's[S] life, his qualities and
miracles are described in every detail. This book is highly admired
throughout the Muslim world and is quick to acquaint the reader
with the true stature of the Prophet[S].

Ash-Shifa gathers together all that is necessary to acquaint the reader with the true stature of the prophet[S], with esteem and respect which is due to him, and with the verdict regarding anyone who dares not fulfil what his stature demands or who attempts to denigrate his supreme status - even by as much as a nail pairing.

18.   Tafsir Al Jalalayn

Tafseer – *authored by Imam Jalal Uddin Muhammad bin Ahmad al-Mahalli (791 - 864 AH, 1389-1459 CE) and Imam Abdul Rahman bin Abu Bakr bin Muhammad bin Sabiq al-din Jalaluddin al Suyuti (849 – 911 AH, 1445-1505 CE)*

Tafsir al-Jalalayn, meaning 'The Commentary of the Two Jalals' is named after its two authors: Jalalu'd-Din al-Mahalli, who wrote half of it, and his student, Jalalu'd-Din as-Suyuti, one of the greatest Muslim scholars, who completed it after al-Mahalli's death. He was raised an orphan and he was a *mujtahid*, a prolific writer, scientist, historian and master of hadith and Islamic sciences.

For half a millennium Tafsir al-Jalalayn has been considered the essential first step in the study of the meanings of the Qur'an by teachers and students throughout the Islamic world, although it is among the shortest and simplest .of the 'complete commentaries', it is at the same time both wide-ranging and profound.

19.   Tabaqat Al-Shafi'iyah Al-Kubra

Collection of ahadith and biographies - *compiled by Imam Tajud-Din 'Abd Al-Wahhab bin 'Alibin 'Abd al-Kafi al Subki (673 – 756 AH, 1275 – 1355 CE)*

Taj al-Din wrote three different works on this same subject, a large work called al-Tabaqt al-Kubra, a more condensed edition, called al-Tabaqt al-Wusta, and a still more condensed edition called al-Tabaqat al-Sughra. These Tabaqat by Taj al-Din have the fame of being the best biographies on Shafi'ite scholars ever written.

Al-Tabaqat al-Kubra, or the great Tabaqat, is a very copious work. Imam Taj al-Din al-Subki ('Abd al-Wahhab b. 'Ali b. 'Abd al-Kafi, Abi Nasr) was a Shafi'i jurist who said about himself, 'I am among those individuals who if they hear something virtuous endeavor to spread it; if they see something questionable endeavor to hide it; and if they witness good in people that would move eyes to tears, endeavour to attach their hearts to it.'

Taj al-Din al-Subki, the author of the Mu'id al-Ni'am wa Mubid al-Niqam, belongs to a large family of al-Subkis, whose members during the seventh and eighth century A.H. made themselves renowned, not only for their learning, high positions as qadis, jurists, consultants, professors, preachers, and writers, but also for their high personal qualities.

20. Al-Bidaya Wanihayya

History – authored by Abu al Fida Imad-adeen Ismaeel bin 'Umar bin kathir bin Daood bin Kathir bin Dir (702 – 774 AH, 1301 – 1373 CE, 8 volumes)

The Classical work Al-Bidayah wan-Nihayah (The Beginning and the End) or Tarikh ibn Kathir (the history book of Ibn Kathir). One of the most comprehensive sources of Islamic history. The beginning of creation and the sending of man upon the earth, Stories of the past Prophets, Seerah of the Prophet Muhammad[S], the times of the Sahaba (Companions), and history up to time of author (768 AH). The last volume records predictions of future events such as signs of the day of judgment *Qiyamah, Barzakh, Jannah & Jahannam.*

Therefore, al Bidayah wan Nihaayah is an excellent reference on the history of the prophets, seerah, the history of early Islam and the history of *al-Shaam* and Iraq up until the year 768H.

The Shade Of The Qur'an is more than 'just another' commentary, yet it is not too over-reaching or outlandish to be a completely new interpretation. It is an earnest, sincere and sober look at man's contemporary achievements and difficulties in the light of the message of the Qur'an. It is an effort to vigorously explore its rich wisdom, and expand its invaluable guidance for the benefit of an increasingly 'sophisticated' , yet highly perplexed modern society. The work, which is by far Sayyid Qutb's largest and most profound, spans the whole of the text of the Qur'an. It was written, and partly re-written, over a period of more than 15 years, most of which the author had spent in Egyptian prisons, during the 1950s and 1960s. In it is embedded Sayyid Qutb's insight, highly esteemed intellectual vigour, and his widely-acclaimed literary prowess. In The Shade Of The Qur'an has been universally recognized as an outstanding contribution to Islamic thought and scholarship, to which students and scholars, as well as contemporary Islamic revivalist movements all over the world, owe a great deal. Now that it is available in English, it will continue to enlighten and inspire millions more.

22.   Tafsir al-Kabir

Tafseer – authored by Abu 'Abdullah Muhammad ibn 'Umar bin al-Husayn al-Taymi al-Bakri-al-Tabaristani Fakhr-ud-din al Razi (543 - 606 AH, 1149-1209 CE, 17 volumes)

Written by Imam Fakhruddin Razi. This is a classical *Tafseer*, published in 32 volumes, written by a famous Sunni Imam and scholar *hazrat Imam* Fakhr al-Din Razi[R]. The real name of this *Tafseer* is Mafateeh al-Ghayb, but is more popular with the name "Tafseer al-Kabir" due to its huge size. It is said that Imam Razi wrote this *Tafseer* himself up to Surah al-Fath when he died. After his death, the remaining part of the tafseer, from Surah al-Fatiha to the end, was completed by Qadi Shihab al-Din ibn Khalil al-Khawli al-Dimashqi (died 639 *Hijrah*) or Shaykh Najm al-Din Ahmad ibn Muhammad al-Qamuli (died 777 *Hijrah*). (Kashaf al-Zunun v. 2, p. 477). He was a great debater, purifying peoples beliefs their deviations.

23.   Majma' al-Zawa'id

Collection of Ahadith - *Compiled by 'Ali bin Abu Bakr al-Haythami (735 – 807 AH, 1335—1404 CE)*

This collection compiles the 'unique' *hadith* of earlier primary collections. Majma al-Zawa'id is a prominent example of the al-zawa'id methodology of *hadith* compilation. It contains *hadith* extracted from Musnad of Ahmad ibn Hanbal, the Musnad by Abu Ya'la al-Mawsili, the Musnad of Abu Bakr al-Bazzar, and three of al-Tabarani's collections: Al-Mu'jam al-Kabir, Al-Mu'jam Al-Awsat and Al-Mu'jam As-Saghir.

The *hadith* gathered by al-Haythami are those not found in the six canonical *hadith* collections: Sahih Bukhari, Sahih Muslim, Sunan al-Sughra, Sunan Abu Daood, Sunan al-Tirmithi and Sunan Ibn Majah. It is considered secondary because it was collected from previous *hadith* collections and does not include the isnad of the *hadith*. In spite of the fact that its source books are primarily arranged as *musnads*, Majma' al-Zawa'id is arranged in the manner of a *sunan* collection – by topical chapter titles relating to jurisprudence. The author provides commentary on the authenticity of each *hadith* and evaluates some of the narrators.

24.   Fat-hul Baari

Explanation of Bukhari – *authored by Abul Fadli Ahmad bin 'Ali bin Muhammad bin Hajr Al-Kinaani Al-Asqalaani (773 – 852 AH, 1372 – 1448 CE, 13 volumes)*

His name is Ahmad Ibn 'Ali Ibn Muhammad Ibn Muhammad 'Ali Al-Kinaani Al-Asqalaani. His great grandparents lived in Asqalaan where they entered it in the year 583 Hijri. The word Hajar is the name of one of his grandfathers. His Kunya is Abul-Fadl and his Laqab is Shihaabuddin. This city Asqalaan is found in Palestine in Ghazza. Ibn Hajar was born on the 12th of Sha'baan, 773 Hijri. Ibn Hajar was an orphan.

In 796 Hijri, Ibn Hajar started to turn to knowledge with even more enthusiasm and dedication then before. He stated, "The veil between me and knowledge was removed and the doors were opened for me to learn with great and strong resolve". He was able to acquire much knowledge and was blessed by Allah[swt] in this regard. He would travel extensively during his days of learning to seek knowledge from the scholars. Ibn Hajar was well known for his piety and his being detached from worldly possessions . The scholars of Islam gave Ibn Hajar precedence and honoured him. One scholar said about him, that he was one of the great scholars our past, he was the Leader of The Believers in regards to hadith, and he was the most knowledgeable scholar of his time. His great book Fat h ul-Bari, is known as a dictionary of the Sunnah, rather it is a dictionary of all the Islamic Sciences, quenching the thirst of all seekers of knowledge.

Fath Al-Bari is Ibn Hajar's most famous book, he also wrote books concerning the narrators mentioned in the six books (Kutub-us-Sitta). He has books in all the various Islamic Sciences such as *Hadith*, *Tafseer*, *Uloom-ul-Qur'an*. On Tuesday 14th of *Dhul-Hijjah* the year 852 *Hijri*, he became ill, such that Saturday 18th of the same month, he passed away in Cairo (may Allah have mercy on his soul).

25.   Tafseer ibn Katheer

Tafseer – *authored by Abu al Fida Imad-adeen Ismaeel bin 'Umar bin kathir bin Daood bin Kathir bin Dir (702 – 774 AH, 1301 – 1373 CE)*

Ibn Kathir wrote a famous commentary on the Qur'an named Tafsir al-Qur'an al-'Adhim which linked certain *ahadith* or sayings of Muhammad, and sayings of the *sahabah* to verses of the Qur'an, in explanation. He is the respected Imam, Abu Al-Fida', `Imad Ad-Din Isma il bin 'Umar bin Kathir Al-Qurashi Al-Busrawi - Busraian in origin; Dimashqi in training, learning and residence.Ibn Kathir was born in the city of Busra in 701 H. His father was the Friday speaker of the village, but he died while Ibn Kathir was only four years old. Ibn Kathir's brother, Shaykh Abdul-Wahhab, reared him and taught him until he moved to Damascus in 706 H., when he was five years old.

Tafsir ibn Kathir is famous all over the Muslim world, and among Muslims in the Western world is one of the most widely used explanations of the Qur'an today. Ibn Kathir was renowned for his great memory regarding the sayings of Muhammad and the entire Qur'an. Ibn Kathir is known as a *qadi*, a master scholar of history, also a *muhaddith* and a *mufassir* (Qur'anic commentator). Ibn Kathir saw himself as a Shafi'i scholar. Al-Hafiz Ibn Hajar Al-Asgalani said, "Ibn Kathir lost his sight just before his life ended. He died in Damascus in 774 H. May Allah grant mercy upon Ibn Kathir and make him among the residents of His Paradise.

26.   Tabarani (Al-Mu'jam al-Kabir – the great dictionary)

Collection of Ahadith - Compiled by Abul Qasim Sulaiman bin Ahmad bin at-Tabarani (260 – 360 AH, 873 – 970 CE, 20,967 ahadith + 1,869)

This is one of the great specialists of *hadith* the Ummah. He is the author of Mu'jam ul Kabir is a collection of famous hadith and often used by scholars, but that does not appear, however, amongst the six major works great hadith that are sahih Al Bukhari, Muslim, the Sunan Abu Dawud, the Sunan Tirmithi, Sunan Anasai and Sunan Ibn Majah. He also authored, Al-Mu'jam Al-Awsat and Al-Mu'jam As-Saghir.

Although remarkable in hadith sciences, he was also a scholar in Qur'anic exegesis, Shafi'i fiqh, kalam, spirituality, history and many other fields of science. He was also ascetic, and strictly following the *Sunnah* of the Messenger of Allah. Imam Al Shams Ud Din Ibn Khallikan[R] made his biography with these words: 'Abul Qasim Ibn Sulayman Ahmad Ibn Ayyub Ibn Mutayr Lakhmi At Tabarani was the Imam of *huffaadh* of his time. After travelling to Syria to collect *ahadith* the Prophet[S] he then travelled well over 33 years, covering Iraq, Hijaz, Yemen, Egypt and various cities of Mesopotamia (Iraq). His collection is so called as he arranges the *ahadith* alphabetically by the narrator (i.e. each chapter is a *musnad*).

The amount of *ahadith* he learned orally was very important and the number of people from whom he learned approaching a thousand. He wrote a few books all useful and full of lessons. Hafith Abu Nu'aym and many others summoned him as an authority. He was born in Tabariyyah (Tiberias) in Syria and had settled in Isfahan until his death, which occurred on Saturday 28 *Dhul Qa'dah* year 360 AH, when he was nearly 100 years.

Some said he died during the month of *Shawwal*. He was buried near the tomb of Hamamah Ad Dawsi, one of the Companions of the Prophet[S]. At-Tabarani means one who is from Tabariyyah, while *Attabari* means, as we have already said, the native Tabaristan. Lakhmi denotes a descendant of Al Lakhm, whose real name was Malik Ibn 'Adi.

27.   Al-Mawaahibul ladunya bil minah al Muhammadiyyah (Prophet Muhammad's[S] gift to the world)

Book of Seerah – authored by Shaikh Ahmad bin Muhammad bin Abi Bakr bin Abi Malik bin Ahmad al-Qastalaani. (851 - 923 AH, 1447 – 1517 CE)

A *hafith* of Qur'an, one of his teachers being ibn Hajar Asqalaani and another being Zakariya al-Ansari. He wrote a 10 volume detailed explanation of *Sahih* al Bukhari. Thus, with tremendous knowledge of Qur'an and *ahadith*, he compiled this concise and detailed 3 volume book on *seerah* using Qur'an and *ahadith* to prove and explain every point. He also quotes conversations between great *fuqahaa* of the past such as Imam Malik and Imam Shafi' and the *salaf*. Unfortunately, like many books of that era, it is currently difficult to reference sections except by volume, chapter and page. We have referenced the Lebanese edition, published 2009 by *Dar-ul-kutub al 'Ilmiyyah*.

28. Roohul Bayan (Soul of the speech)

Tafseer – authored by Imam Shaikh Isma'eel Haqqi bin Mustafa al-Islamabuli al-Hanafi al-Khalwati al-Mawla Abu Fadda-i al-Burusi mutasawif a- mufassir (1063 - 1127 AH, 1653– 1715 CE, 10 volumes)

This famous Turkish *Mufassir* wrote this momentous work amongst many other books in Arabic and Turkish. These were as diverse as *Tasawwuf* and Arabic Etymology such as Al-'Araba'oona Haditha (40 hadith), Kitabu-al-khitaab (*Tasawwuf*), Rislaaltul Khalila (*Tasawwuf*). His *tafseer* is 10 volumes and is world famous amongst *'Ulema*.

29. At-Targheeb wat-Tarheeb (Warnings and Benefits)

Collection of ahadith – authored by Imam al Haafidh Zakiyyuddin Abu 'Atheem bin 'Abdi al-Qawee al-Mundhir (581 – 656 AH, 1185 – 1258 CE)

This popular and famous collection deals with virtues and various good deeds as well as warnings collated by a master of *ahadith*. It is highly useful to anyone requiring knowledge about the same from *ahadith* collected from different books of *ahadith*.

30. Al Muwatta (The Approved)

Collection of ahadith – compiled by Abu 'Abdullahi Malik bin Anas bin Malik bin Abu Amir bin Amr al-haarith bin ghayman bin khudain bin amri bin haarith al asbahi (93 – 179 AH, 711 – 795 CE, 1,891 ahadith)

A powerful and famous Muslim Jurist and the Imam of the 'Maliki' school. He was known as the Imam of Medina in his time and one of the most highly respected scholars of Fiqh in the *sunni* school. His generosity and love for the Prophet[S] is legendary. Humble, god-fearing, uncompromising and sincere. He would never relate a *hadith* without *wudu* and would perfume the air out of love and respect. His purpose for this compilation was to collate and categorise *ahadith* in relation to *fiqh*. Imam Malik[R] stated that he gave his book to 70 Jurists of Medina at the time and they all unanimously approved it, hence the title al-Muwatta (the Approved). Imam Shaf'i stated that after the Holy Qur'an, this book was the most authentic and he had memorised it by heart. This was one of the first comprehensive collection of *ahadith*.

31. Hilyatul Awliyaa wa Tabaqatul Asfiyah
(Adornment of the saints and the ranks of the spiritual elite)

Collection of stories of the pious – *authored by Shaikh Abul Mu'een Ahmad Asfahani (336 - 430 AH, 948 – 1038 CE)*

This book quotes sayings of over 200 *awliya ikram* (*sahaba*, *tabi'een* and *taba tabi'een*) in the first 3 generations of the *ummah*.

32. Minhaj us Sunnah

Discussion between different Muslim groups Authored by Ibne Taymiyyah (661 – 728 AH, 1263 – 1328 CE).

This book is based upon extensive discussions between different groups.

33. Tafsir al Tabari

Tafseer. Authored byAbu Ja'far Muhammad bin Jarir al Tabari (224 – 310 AH, 838 – 923 CE).

Imam Tabari's most famous works are his tafseer and Tarikh al Rasool wa al Muluk (history of the prophets and the kings). He was eloquent, independent and deeply knowledgeable and his *tafseer* was utilised extensively by Imam Baghwi, Imam Suyuti and Ibne Katheer.

Appendix 3

Glossary of Arabic Terms

Abdaal/Qutb/Ghawth	Lofty rank of the friends of Allah
Abwaab	Books or chapters (plural of *baab*)
Aqaaid	Beliefs
A'maru/Ya'maru	Build, shape or maintain
Al-Jam'a	The majority
A.H.	After Hijri
Ahadith	Plural of *hadith* (sayings and traditions of the Prophet[S])
Ahlus sunnah wal jam'a	People of the sunnah and majority
Ahlul Bid'ah wal firqqah	People of (bad) innovation and sects
Auliya Ikram	Noble friends of Allah
Athaan	Call to prayer
Aqeeqah	Symbolizes the sacrifice offered on the seventh day after child's birth
Baab	Book or chapter (plural – *abwaab*))
Barakah	Blessing or reward
Bid'ah	Innovation (in religion)
Bay'ah	Oath of allegiance
Barzakh	Afterlife (literally – barrier)
Basharun mithlukum	Should be understood as 'a man for your example'
C.E.	Christian Era
Deen	Religion
Du'a	Supplication / prayer

Eesal-e-thawaab	passing rewards to the deceased
Fatwas	Ruling
fadaail a'maal	Extra actions of devotion
Fard	Compulsory
Ghawth/Abdaal/Qutb	Lofty rank of the friends of Allah
Giyarwee	Eleven (urdu)
Habashi	Ethiopian
Hajj	Holy pilgrimage
Haji	One who has done hajj
Haadir and Naathir	Omnipresent
Hazrat	Honourable
Halal	Allowed/ Permissible (opposite of *haram*)
Haram	Forbidden (opposite of *halal*)
Haramain	*Masjid Haram* and *Msjid Nabwi*[S]
Hadith	Saying (and traditions) of the Prophet[S]
Ijtihad	A Scholar making personal effort and undertaking research to form an opinion or opinions on a point or points of Islamic Law. Only experts in Islamic Sciences can undertake this process.
Ilah	God or deity
Imaan	Faith
Isra	Journey (typically referring to the night journey from Makkah *Mukarramah* to Al Aqsa)
Jahiliyyah	Ignorance
Jannah	Paradise (literal-Garden)
Jahannam	Hellfire (literal- Pit)

Kafir	Disbeliever
Karamat	Miracles (or blessings)
Kuffar	Plural of *kafir (one who disbelieves)*
Kalimah Tayyibah	the first *kalimah (There is no god but Allah Muhammad is his Messenger[s])*
Khatam	Reading and completing the whole Qur'an
Karamat	Marvel or miracle
Lailatul Qadr	Night of power (27th Ramadan)
Maudu'	Fabricated (*hadith*)
Mu-athin	One who calls for prayer (*athaan*)
Muhaddith	Scholar of traditions (*Hadith*)
Muhaditheen	Plural of *Muhaddith*
Mukarramah	Noble (usually Makkah *Mukarramah* - 'noble city of Makkah')
Mushrik	Polytheist
Mu'jizah	MIracles
Mushrikeen	Plural of *mushrik* (one who associates others with Allah)
Mutlaq	Not restricted to time
Mandub	Permissible (*halal*)
Musnad	According to the narrator (literally 'supported')
Mustahab	Reward if done
Mizaar	Grave of a Muslim saint (visited by Muslims)
Mashaaikh	Spiritual guides, plural of *shaykh*
Madhab	School of thought

Murshid / Peer / Shaikh	Spiritual guide
Nidaa	Calling (a term of grammar)
Peer / Shaikh / Murshid	Spiritual guide
Qabr	Grave
Qurratu Aini bika Ya Rasoolallah[S]	Yaa Rasoolallah[S], you are the coolness of my eyes
Qutb/Abdaal/ Ghawth	Lofty rank of the friends of Allah
Rak'ah	One cycle of ritual prayer
Ruqyah	Amulet, spell, charm, magic or incantation
Salah	Prayer
Sahaba Ikraaam	Noble companions
Sahih Sitta	'Six authentic' (commonly referred to Bukhari, Muslim, Tirmithi, Abu Daood, Ibne Majah & Nisaai books on *ahadith*)
Salaat Istisqaa	Prayer for rain
Salaat and salaam	Blessings and salutation
Sajdah	Prostration
Sayyidina	Our master or respected
Seerah	History of the life of the Prophet[S].
Shaahid	Witness
Shahaadah	Testimony (of faith)
Shawl/hijab	Traditional covering for Muslim women
Shaitan	The devil
Shari'ah	Islamic law (literally – way to the water)
Sharh	Explanation

Shaikh / pir / murshid	Spiritual guide
Sufi	Pious people who practice *tasawwuf* (spirituality)
Sunan	Prophetic traditions (plural of *sunnah*)
Sunnah	Prophetic tradition of the Prophet Muhammad[S] (his sayings, actions and approvals)
Surah	Chapter in the holy Qur'an
Tafseer	Commentary of the holy Qur'an
Taqbeelul Ibhaamain	Kissing ones thumbs & rubbing on one's eyes when hearing the name of Prophet Muhammad[S]
Taqleed	Imitating / following
Taqleed Shakhsi	Following without question
Taqwa	God-consciousness, God-fearing, piety
Tawaaf	Circulating around kaaba 7 times
Tawassul	Help from an intermediary
Taweeth	Written du'a from Qur'an or hadith for treatment
Tawheed	Monotheism
thalathiaat ahadith	Ahadith with only 3 narrators in the chain. Thus these are likely to be highly authentic.
Thikr	Remembrance
'Ulema	Scholars
Ummah	Nation (of Muslims)
'Urs	Restful, blissful sleep
Waajib	Compulsory as proved by presumptive evidence
Wali Allah	Friend of Allah

Waseelah	Intermediary
Walliyan Murshida	guiding teacher
Waliyyatullah	Friend of Allah^{swt} (female)
Wudu	Ritual ablution
Zaahid	one who denounces the world
<u>A</u>	*'Alaihis salaam* (On him be peace)
<u>R</u>	*Radyallaahu 'an hu* (May Allah be pleased with him – for companions)
<u>R</u>	*Rahmatullaa 'alaiy* (May Allah's mercy be upon him – for saints and pious people)
<u>S</u>	*Sal lal laahu 'alaihi wa sallam* (peace and blessings be upon him)
<u>swt</u>	*Subhaa nahu wa ta 'aalaa* (Glory be to Him the high)

Appendix 4

Additional References

This section provides additional references for completeness where denoted within the main text. Please note that references may vary slightly from different publishers for which we have no control.

Reference Nomenclature:

(Holy Qur'an 15:5)	-	*Holy Qur'an, surah 1 5, verse 5*
HQ	-	*Holy Qur'an*
Bukhari 93:502	-	*Sahih al-Bukhari, book/chapter 93 hadith nr 502*
Tirmithi 2,173	-	*Hadith number 2,173 (normally counted from the beginning, but numbers may vary slightly for different published versions)*
'vol2 p240 ch12'	-	*Volume 2 page 240 chapter 12*
'...'	-	*Means text omitted due to space but without affecting meaning*

References:

[1]   *Hassan and Sahih, Musnad Ahmad bin hanbal 4:138 p17,246-7, Umdatus-saalik, Imam Bukhari in Tarikhul Kabeer, Al-Hakeem 1:313). (Chapter 6)*

[2]   *Volume 2, page 17. It can also be found in Tirmithi, Daarimi, and Tabarani. There is another, similar hadith on the same page. (Chapter 8)*

[3]   *Also in Tirmithi 3,543 & 3,628 but with a slightly different wording. (Chapter 9)*

[4]   *Imam Abdul Rahman bin Abu Bakr bin Muhammad bin Sabiq al-din Jalaluddin al Suyuti^R in his book Kitabut-tanweer fi maulad basheerin-nazeer, page 25. (Chapter 13)*

[5]   *Abu Nu'aym in hisDala'il an-Nubuwwa (p. 6), Daylami (Musnad Firdaws, 3:282 -4850 and 4:411 -7190), Ibn 'Adiyy (Kamil,*

3:919, 1209), Tabari (Tafsir, 15:10, 21:125-26), Baghawi (Tafsir, 3:508). (Chapter 14)

[6]   *Also Tabarani 8:290, Daarimi 2:170 and others with similar words. (Chapter 17)*

[7]   Also in *Abu Nu'aym in his Dala'il an-Nubuwwa (p. 6), Daylami (MusThunad Firdaws, 3:282 -4850 and 4:411 -7190), Ibn 'Adiyy (Kamil, 3:919, 1209), Tabari (Tafsir, 15:10, 21:125-26), Baghawi (Tafsir, 3:508). (Chapter 18)*

[8]   *Narrated by Ubadah ibn as-Samit. Allah's Messenger[S] said: 'The first thing which Allah created was the 'Pen'. He Commanded it to write. It asked: 'What should I write?' The Lord Most Exalted Said: 'Write the Decree (al-Qadr).' So it wrote <u>what had happened</u> and what was going to happen up to eternity. (Tirmithi 2,162)*

   Also: The first thing which Allah created was the Pen, and He said to it, 'Write.' It responded, 'What should I write?' He said, 'Write everything that will occur until the Day of Resurrection.' (Abu Daood 4,700, Tirmithi 3,330, Ahmad 22,768) (Chapter 18).

[9]   *Mawahib Lidunya Volume 2, chapter on Mu'jizaat (miracles), page 240. Also in Tabari. Also narrated by Abu Hafs bin Shaheen (Chapter 19)*

[10]   *Al-Khairatul Hassan **Vol 1** Page 38, Tareekh Khateeb-e-Baghdadi Vol 1 Page 123, Raddul Mukhrat Vol 1 Page 38, Narrated by al-Khatib in Tarikh Baghdad (1:123) cf. al-Kawthari in his Maqalat (p. 453) and by Ibn Abi al-Wafa in Tabaqat al-Hanafiyya (p. 519) through al-Ghaznawi. Imam al-Haytami cites it in the thirty-fifth chapter of his book on Imam Abu Hanifa entitled al-Khayrat al- Hisan. (Chapter 21 & 25)*

[11]   *Safa & marwah (name of blessed hills near the Ka'bah), Haramain (Masjid haram and nabwi shareefain), jannatul Baqi (graveyard adjacent to Masjid Nabwi shareef) , Arafa (plain where Muslims gather on Hajj) , Muzdalifa (area where Muslims gather after Hajj), Al-Aqsaa (Masjid in Jerusalem where Prophet MuhammadS ascended to heavens and also the first Qibla), maqaame-ibraheem ('station of IbrahimA' – place where IbrahimA stood whilst constructing the Ka'ba. It is a miraculous stone that holds his blessed footprint), hajre-aswad (black stone fixed into the Ka'ba). (Chapter 25)*

119

[12]   *Albadaya wan nahaya vol4 p45, Abdur Razzaq al-musnaf :*
        3:573 2.. Aini , Umdat-ul-Qari, 8:70 3.. Tabari, Jami Al-Quran,
        13:142 4.. Imam Suyuti, Dur-ul-Mansoor, 4:641 5. Ibn-e-Kathir,
        tafseer-ul-Quran-ul-Azeem. Radd al-Muhtar (also famous as
        Hashiyat Ibn Abidin and, in the Indian subcontinent, as Shami)
        also contains a prophetic tradition in Vol. 1, Baabu Ziyaaratil-
        Quboor to show that the Holy Prophet^S used to visit Uhud
        annually. (Chapter 21)

[13]   *Recorded by Hakim at-Tirmithi in Nawadir (Asl Nr 123) and*
        Khatm al-Awliya (p. 443), Abu Nu'aym in his Hilya (2:24, 81)
        and Ma'rifat as-Sahaba (5:2810 Nr3,079), ibn 'Asakir in his
        Tarikh (3:200), Ruyani in his Musnad (3:335), Abu Muhammad
        al-Khallal in Karamat al-Awliya', ibn al-Athir in his Usd al-
        Ghaba (5:124), and others. See also: ibn Hajar"s Isaba fi Tamyiz
        as-Sahaba (6:550). (Chapter 31)

[14]   *Recorded by Tabarani in Mu'jam Kabir, Ibn 'Asakir (1:277,*
        298), Bazzar, and others. Sahih according to Suyuti and Munawi,
        and Haythami (10:63 Nr 16,673) said he did not know one of the
        narrators, but the rest are of the Sahih. A similar hadith was also
        recorded by Tabarani in his Kabir (18:65) and Ibn 'Asakir
        (1:290) on the authority of 'Awf ibn Malik, which is sound
        (Hasan) according to Munawi, and thru Ibn Mas'ud (M. Kabir
        10:181 – also by Abu Nu'aym in Hilya 4:173-74). Cf. Suyuti's
        Jami' as-Saghir (Nr 3,034, "Hassan"). (Chapter 31)

[15]   *Similar narration in Abu Daood 3,884. Imam Qurtubi*
        Rahmatullah wrote in detail about both types of Ahadith
        concerning Ta'weeth: 'The Ta'weeth that are forbidden are those
        from the time of ignorance, those which are Satanic and contain
        an element of Shirk'. (Mantar, Voodoo and Magic etc.) The
        Ta'weeth, which are permitted are those written with Du'as,
        which are evident from Qur'an and Ahadith only. (Chapter 32)

[16]   *Dhakwan said: I said to 'A'ishah, 'Who named 'Umar "al-*
        Farooq"?' She said, 'The Prophet, may Allah bless him and grant
        him peace.' Ibn 'Abbas, may Allah be pleased with them both,
        said: When 'Umar accepted Islam, then Jibraeel descended and
        said, 'Muhammad, the inhabitants of heaven rejoice in 'Umar's
        acceptance of Islam." Ibn 'Abbas, may Allah be pleased with them
        both, said: When 'Umar accepted Islam, the idolators said, 'The
        people have been split in half from us today,' and Allah revealed,

'O Prophet, Allah is enough for you; and whoever follows you of the believers.' (Qur'an 8: 64). (taken from The History of the Khalifahs by Jalal ad-Din as-Suyuti) (Chapter 33).

[17] *Also, Ikrima, Muhammad ibn Ka`b al-Qurazi, Rabi` ibn Anas and the Tafsirs Ibn Kathir (2:656) and al-Suyuti's al-Durr al-Manthur (3:315). (Chapter 34)*

[18] *Muslim 2,700, Muwatta 3,791, Nisaai 953 Ahmad 11,463 Ibn-Abi-Shaibah. (Chapter 35)*

[19] *The name of that companion was Abdullah Zul-Bujadain[R]. (Chapter 35)*

[20] *Nabi (Prophet), Rasool (Messenger), Ansaar (Helpers), Muhajiroon (Emigrants), Muslim (one who submits), Mu'min (believer), shuhadaa (martyrs), siddiqeen (truthful ones), saaliheen (righteous), muttaqeen (pious), awliyaa (friends of Allah), 'ulemaa (Islamic scholars), Muhsineen (righteous), Imam (leader)...etc. Chapter 39.*

[21] *Zurqani in Sharah Mawahib ul Laduniyah Volume 001, Page No. 89-91, Ajluni in Kashf al-Khafa Volume 001, Page No. 311, Hadith Number 827,Halabi in his Sirah Volume 001, Page No. 50,Ashraf Ali Thanvi in Nashar ut-Tib Volume 001, Page No. 13, Musannaf Abdur Razaq, al-Juz al-Mafqud min al-Juz al-Awwal min al-Musannaf Abdur Razaq, Page No. 99, Hadith Number 18). (Appendix 1)*

[22] The full hadith is: *Narrated `Umar[R], the Prophet[S] said, 'When Adam[A] committed his mistake he said: 'O my Lord, I am asking you to forgive me by the sake of Muhammad[S].' Allah said, 'O Adam, and how do you know about Muhammad whom I have not yet created (in bodily form)?' Adam replied, 'O my Lord, after You created me with your hand and breathed into me Your Spirit, I raised my head and saw written on the heights of the Throne: 'Laa ilaaha illallah Muhammadur rasoo lullah'. I understood that You would not place next to Your Name but the most beloved of your creation.' Allah said, 'O Adam, I have forgiven you, and were it not for Muhammad[S] I would not have created you.' (Mustadrak 2:672, 4,228) (Chapter 28)*

* * * * * *

121